How to Be a Pastor

"Previous generations of pastors excelled as doctors of the soul. They modeled the priority of not only word-ministry but congregational soul care. In *How to Be a Pastor*, nineteenth-century pastor Theodore Cuyler personifies the details of shepherding the local church. In a short, readable volume, Cuyler strips away the clutter that can distract pastors to identify specific, doable ways to genuinely shepherd the flock. I'll be eagerly recommending this book to pastors and students as a short primer on faithful pastoral work."

—PHIL A. NEWTON, director of pastoral
care and mentoring, Pillar Network

"In an age of the greatest de-churching movement in American history, we pastors need encouragement and guidance. This book gives us much of what we need. As popular as he was in the nineteenth century, Theodore Cuyler is not well known today. But he should be. His pastoral ministry had a profound, godly influence on his congregation precisely because of his godly character and his commitment to pastoral fundamentals. This book boils it all down to the basics. Pastors, get it. Read it."

—SANDY WILLSON, interim president, The Gospel Coalition

"This profoundly heartwarming book will refresh the spirits of many pastors and aspiring pastors. It comes from another age and a different culture. But it breathes the love of the Savior through the affections of the pastor. I warmly commend this beautiful book to pastors and all who care about pastoral leadership in our churches."

—CHRISTOPHER ASH, writer in residence,
Tyndale House, Cambridge

"*How to Be a Pastor* reminds every one of us with stunning clarity what the true timeless call of a pastor is—to care for souls. Every pastor and aspiring pastor should read this book and keep it close."

—**BRIAN CROFT**, executive director, Practical Shepherding

"There are two things every pastor must do: preach the word and tend the flock. This book is the story of one man who did both things well in the midst of a busy urban ministry marked by prayer, soul winning, and personal pastoral care. An inspiring read for every pastor and for every young minister preparing to become one."

—**TIMOTHY GEORGE**, distinguished professor, Beeson Divinity School

How to Be a Pastor

Wisdom from the Past for Pastors in the Present

Theodore L. Cuyler

Edited by
Ray Van Neste and Justin Wainscott

WIPF & STOCK · Eugene, Oregon

Wipf & Stock
An Imprint of Wipf and Stock Publishers
199 W. 8th Ave., Suite 3
Eugene, OR 97401

www.wipfandstock.com

PAPERBACK ISBN: 979-8-3852-0512-7
HARDCOVER ISBN: 979-8-3852-0513-4
EBOOK ISBN: 979-8-3852-0514-1

VERSION NUMBER 01/03/24

Unless otherwise noted, all scriptures are from the KING JAMES VER-
SION, public domain.

To the young ministers of the Lord Jesus Christ

in all Christian denominations,

this little volume

is lovingly inscribed.

(Theodore Cuyler, 1890)

Contents

Acknowledgements

WE ARE GRATEFUL FOR the labors of Theodore Cuyler and for the privilege of bringing his work to light for a new generation of pastors.

We also want to thank everyone at Wipf and Stock for their willingness to see the value in this project and for their help in reproducing this volume.

We appreciate all that our assistant, Mrs. Julie Chhim, did to aid us in this work; and we are thankful for the encouragement and support we receive from our colleagues in the School of Theology and Missions at Union University and from our president, Dr. Dub Oliver, as well as our provost, Dr. John Netland. We are grateful to serve at an institution that seeks to embody the pastoral vision that Cuyler articulates.

I (Ray) am grateful for friendships the Lord provides. Producing a new edition of Cuyler's *How to Be a Pastor* was a dream of mine, but it was just a dream until Justin Wainscott joined me as a colleague at Union University. Justin brought renewed energy to the project, resulting in the dream becoming a reality.

I am also grateful to Fellowship Baptist in Kenosha, WI, the first church I served as pastor, as they took a chance on a young pastor and loved my wife and me. Peterhead Baptist and International Baptist were delightful places of ministry during my family's time in Scotland, where in fellowship with those saints my understanding of pastoral ministry grew. Then it was at Cornerstone

Acknowledgements

Community Church where I first really pursued the vision of pastoral ministry articulated here, and I am grateful for their receptivity and support.

Lastly, I am thankful as always for my family, the "little church in my own home," for their encouragement and support. My children—Nathan, Matthew, Jonathan, Benjamin, Abigail, Timothy—now several of them with wives and children of their own, continue to be sources of great joy. My wife, Tammie, supports and encourages me in so many ways since I first asked her to "magnify the LORD with me and let us exalt his name together" (Ps 34:3).

I (Justin) want to add my thanks to Ray for both his friendship and his invitation to join him in this project. It is a joy to labor alongside him and to work together in such ventures.

I also want to express my personal thanks to two men who served as pastoral mentors to me. One is Rev. Bob Elliott, who I had the privilege of serving under and from whom I learned so much about what it means to be a pastor. The other is Dr. Robert Smith, Jr., who has been a father in ministry to me and a wonderful example of how to be a pastor.

I am grateful for the churches I have been privileged to serve in pastoral ministry—First Baptist Somerville, Pleasant Plains Baptist, First Baptist Paducah, and First Baptist Jackson. I appreciate their patience, encouragement, support, and love.

Thank you as well to the pastors of my local church—Gary, Ryan, and Dennis. I am grateful for these men and for their faithful care of the flock.

Finally, I want to thank my family, whom I love. My children—Ella, Graham, and Gavin—are a wonderful gift and a constant joy. And my wife, Anna, blesses me in more ways than I can describe and loves me much better than I deserve: "She is far more precious than jewels. The heart of her husband trusts in her . . ." (Prov 31:10–11).

Introduction

THEODORE CUYLER IS NOT a name widely recognized today. In fact, many of you reading this book may have never even heard of him. But that was not the case in his own day. During his lifetime, he was mentioned in the same breath alongside prominent figures (and acquaintances of his) such as Charles Spurgeon, Dwight Moody, and Horatius Bonar. He was "the celebrated Brooklyn divine" and pastor of the largest Presbyterian congregation in the United States. One Baptist newspaper referred to him, along with Charles Spurgeon, as "two of the world's greatest men." Henry Ward Beecher, another prominent preacher and contemporary of Cuyler's, said of him, "Theodore Cuyler writes the best religious articles of any man alive." And the *N. Y. Tribune* went so far as to say, "Dr. Cuyler has been, himself, almost an ideal pastor."

But the life, ministry, and writings of this "almost . . . ideal pastor" remain largely unknown by pastors today. Therefore, our aim in reproducing this volume is to introduce Cuyler to a new generation of pastors and to share the wealth of wisdom he offers from a long and faithful ministry. In short, we believe that his is a voice worth recovering and worth hearing. Moreover, we believe that he has important things to say about pastoral ministry, things that are often neglected in our own day and age.

In these opening pages, then, we want to introduce you to Cuyler himself and to his work, *How to Be a Pastor*. Additionally, we hope to help you see the value of this volume and why a book on pastoral ministry written in 1890 still has significance well over a century later.

BIOGRAPHICAL SKETCH

Theodore Ledyard Cuyler (1822–1909) spent most of his long life in and around the Northeast. He was born in New York, educated in New Jersey at Princeton University (1841) and Princeton Theological Seminary (1846), and pastored churches in both New Jersey and New York. If his geography was somewhat limited, his friendships, acquaintances, and influence were anything but. Cuyler's circle of friends and acquaintances included a large number of notable figures—Phillips Brooks, Horace Bushnell, Charles Finney, Philip Schaff, and as mentioned above, Horatius Bonar, D. L. Moody, and Charles Spurgeon. Added to that list are prominent political leaders such as President Benjamin Harrison, Vice President Henry Wilson, and Prime Minister William Gladstone. A devoted abolitionist and an outspoken supporter of the Temperance movement, his theological convictions impacted his views on society. His books and articles were widely circulated, and he was elected to the American Philosophical Society as a young man in his thirties. His significance and influence can still be seen today by the park in Brooklyn that bears his name, Cuyler Gore Park.

But what Cuyler was most known for was being a pastor. His first pastorate was in Burlington, New Jersey, a struggling church which he helped revive. Then in 1853, he was called as pastor of the Market Street Dutch Reformed Church in New York City. He served there for seven years before being called in 1860 as pastor of Park Presbyterian Church in Brooklyn. From Park Presbyterian, he oversaw the construction of Lafayette Avenue Presbyterian Church a block away, which was completed in 1862. Under Cuyler's leadership, the newly constructed church became the largest Presbyterian congregation in the United States. He served as pastor of that congregation for thirty years until his retirement in 1890. During his tenure, the church received almost four thousand and five hundred members. And remarkably, almost two thousand of them were new converts who came on profession of faith in Jesus Christ.

Cuyler could not have served a church of that size and of that prominence without being a skilled preacher, a consistent evangelist, and a sound theologian. But what marked his ministry above all was his care for the souls entrusted to him as a pastor. Whether it was ministering to souls under conviction, caring for the sick and dying, or regularly visiting the flock, Cuyler provided a model for the kind of under-shepherd Scripture calls pastors to be. And when it came to ministering to the suffering, he did so from his own experiences with sorrow, having lost his father when he was five and having lost two children in infancy and another when she was only twenty-one.

Over four decades of pastoral experience taught Cuyler much about life, ministry, the church, and human hearts. Those lessons are all on full display in the many books and articles he wrote, including *Heart-life* (1871), *Pointed Papers for the Christian Life* (1879), *God's Light on Dark Clouds* (1882), *The Young Preacher* (1893), *Beulah-Land, or Words of Good Cheer to the Old* (1896), *Well-Built: Plain Talks to Young People* (1898), and *A Model Christian* (1903). But the book that best and most clearly brings together the lessons learned from his many years as a pastor is the work in the following pages, *How to Be a Pastor*—a work that emphasizes the importance of pastors overseeing and caring for souls.

THE VALUE OF *HOW TO BE A PASTOR*

If you are wondering why two Baptists like us would commend the work of a forgotten Presbyterian like Cuyler, there are at least two reasons. Generally speaking, we believe that there is much we have to learn from our brothers and sisters in other Christian traditions. So, just because we may differ with Cuyler on some issues does not mean that we cannot appreciate and learn from him, especially on a matter such as pastoral ministry, which is not uniquely Presbyterian, Baptist, Anglican, Lutheran, etc. But the specific reason we are commending Cuyler and this work of his is because we believe he addresses important and neglected pastoral issues.

We certainly appreciate and value seminary training for pastors. In fact, both of us have spent time teaching in seminary classrooms, and both of us regularly encourage future pastors to attend seminary. But we also recognize that seminary is not intended to teach pastors everything they need to know in order to carry out their calling faithfully and effectively. There are some lessons best learned (perhaps, only learned) outside the classroom at the feet of a wiser, experienced pastor.

But sadly, not every young pastor will have the opportunity to serve under an older, trusted pastor. And that's why a work like Cuyler's *How to Be a Pastor* is so helpful and so needed. It has the potential to serve as something of a stand-in for the personal, practical mentoring that a young pastor needs. And, when young pastors do experience the blessing of being mentored by an older pastor, this book can serve as a wonderful resource in such mentoring relationships. Indeed, this book was originally dedicated to "the young ministers of the Lord Jesus Christ in all Christian denominations," and it was written to "discuss in the most familiar, colloquial, and practical fashion, the everyday duties of a Christian pastor." As Cuyler mentions at the beginning, "[I]f the results of forty-four years of experience and observation shall prove to be of value to others—especially my younger brethren—I shall be thankful."

We believe that Cuyler has good reason to be thankful because we believe his experiences and observations do prove to be of value to younger pastors (and seasoned pastors as well). As already alluded to, one of the reasons we believe his work is so valuable is because of the particular aspects of being a pastor that he stresses. They are aspects that often get ignored in current conversations about pastoral ministry, but they are aspects that previous generations of pastors, generations such as Cuyler's, recognized as worthy of emphasis. Specifically, they emphasized that there is so much more to being a pastor than being in the pulpit (as important as that may be); being a pastor is primarily about being in people's lives—providing faithful, loving, spiritual oversight of the souls under your care.

In reproducing this volume, we hope to help revive a vision of pastoral ministry which upholds the central importance of the oversight of souls (Heb 13:17), the necessity of knowing the individual people in a congregation, being aware of their burdens, struggles, joys, and growth, as well as the necessity of ministering to individuals and not simply speaking from a distance. To be pastored well, people must be known. But too often, pastors (indeed, much of the church) think pastoral ministry is about preaching or strategizing or vision-casting or branding, missing the fact that caring for souls is the center of all else we do as pastors. We preach in order to guard souls, we pray in order to guard souls, we plan, prepare, budget, and everything else for the purpose of guiding souls safely home to the Celestial City.

One of the most common objections we encounter to this vision of ministry is that it is a novel idea or at least an abstract one which is unrealistic in day-to-day ministry. Some who are aware will concede that Richard Baxter did this but no one since then has. Cuyler's *How to Be a Pastor* dispels this objection, providing a wonderful example of this vision of the oversight of souls, following the example of so many before him, including Gregory the Great, Gregory of Nazianzus, Martin Bucer, Samuel Rutherford, Henry Scougal, and John Angell James.

We hope Cuyler's voice from the past will challenge and inspire a new generation of pastors to engage in caring for individual people and not merely to "run a church." This shift can lead to increased health in churches and in pastors across the country.

A TASTE OF WHAT'S TO COME

To give you an idea of the kinds of matters Cuyler addresses in this work, as well as a taste of what you can expect in the pages that follow, this section provides a summary of each chapter along with selected quotes from Cuyler himself. In Chapter 1, "The Importance of Pastoral Labor," Cuyler argues that being a pastor is more than preaching sermons. It requires taking a personal interest in the flock, not neglecting to spend time with the people. "Every pulpit needs to be vitalized by close contact with living people rather than with lifeless books; and the best practical discourses are those which the congregation help their minister prepare."

Chapter 2 turns to a specific aspect of pastoral labor, "Pastoral Visits." Cuyler writes, "Set it down as a prime rule to spend part of every day in circulating among your people. Do not let your library—no, not even your Bible or your sermon study, entice you away from your pastoral duties . . . Set it down as a cardinal principle, my young brother, that if you would interest people in the gospel and interest them in their salvation, you have got to interest *yourself* in them and all that belongs to them."

Another key part of pastoral work, "Visitation of the Sick and Funeral Services," is the subject of Chapter 3. Because there will be many in the church who suffer and some who die, much of a pastor's time will be devoted to visiting the sick and conducting funerals. Cuyler argues that these are not duties to avoid or duties to endure. Rather, they are unique opportunities to show love and compassion: "A pastor should be as quick to hasten to the room of sickness, as an ambulance is to reach a scene of a disaster."

Chapter 4 deals with "The Treatment of the Troubled." As Cuyler wisely states, "A large part of every Christian minister's work must be given to those who are in trouble . . . Bruised hearts are to be bound up; feeble knees to be strengthened; a word in season to be spoken to the weary or the weak or the woebegone . . . In dealing with the afflicted—from whatever cause it come—we must treat them always as scholars in God's school of suffering."

In Chapter 5, "How to Have a Working Church," Cuyler points out that eloquent preaching alone will not lead to an actively serving church. Therefore, he offers five suggestions on how to have an active, working church—suggestions gathered from his forty years of experience and which he shares in hopes that they "may be of value to beginners in the ministry."

Cuyler treats the important but too often neglected topic of "Training Converts" in Chapter 6. So often, much of "the power in the church" fails to be realized because "new converts are not trained into Christian activity from the start." Cuyler shares from his own experiences about how best to train and involve new believers.

In Chapter 7, "Prayer Meetings," he addresses another topic that is so often neglected today. But according to Cuyler, "The prayer meeting may fairly claim to be regarded as second only to the pulpit in the spiritual life of a Christian church . . . a well attended, well conducted prayer meeting is both a joy to the pastor and a wellspring of blessings to the people." Therefore, Cuyler offers specific instructions on how to plan for and ensure such a well conducted prayer meeting. Then Chapter 8, "A Model Prayer Meeting," details what it is like to experience a model prayer meeting—from what is said, what is sung, what is prayed, who participates, and what spirit permeates the gathering.

Chapter 9 is focused on "Revivals." Cuyler writes, "After a long pastoral experience and frequent labors in revivals, I confess that there is much that is utterly mysterious in regard to them. Our God is a sovereign." While he readily admits that revivals are the surprising work of God, he goes on to offer seven specific and helpful bits of advice based on his own experience—everything from preaching to prayer to what to look for and how to speak with inquirers.

Chapter 10, "Drawing the Bow at a Venture," aims to encourage pastors by reminding them that God uses words they have spoken in ways they may never know. Cuyler shares a specific instance from his own experience as an example.

The subject of Chapter 11 is "Where to Be a Pastor," answering the question, "Should a young minister take a large church or a small one for his first pastorate"? Cuyler answers unhesitatingly that he should take the smaller one, and part of the reason why is because of the very nature of the pastoral ministry he describes throughout the previous chapters.

The twelfth and final chapter, "The Joys of the Christian Ministry," contains the farewell discourse Cuyler delivered upon his retirement as pastor of Lafayette Avenue Church. Built around

1 Thess 2:19–20, he reflects on his own four decades of pastoral ministry and the joys he has experienced during them.

EDITORIAL PROCESS

As for the editorial process we used in this book, we have tried as much as possible to let Cuyler speak for himself (in his original voice). Therefore, with only a very few exceptions, the original language has been preserved throughout. The only changes made were simply for the sake of preventing distraction or confusion for a modern reader, and those changes were limited to a few words which no longer carry the same connotation as they did in Cuyler's day. In addition, the spelling of certain words has been updated, and minor grammatical edits have been made (primarily related to the usage of commas and hyphens) to make the work more suitable to a style that readers are accustomed to today. Elsewhere, footnotes have been added to help readers understand references to quotations, names, places, etc. And since Cuyler quoted and alluded to numerous passages of Scripture without providing any references, we have also taken the time to add the specific Scripture references in parentheses throughout the volume. Otherwise, the content looks and sounds just like it did in 1890.

Our aim, then, in this work has not been one of *renovation* but of *restoration*. We have not attempted to "make it our own." Nor we have tried to "knock down walls" and "repurpose" the original for some other use. Instead, we have sought to blow off a century's worth of dust and neglect, clean up and polish what was underneath, and restore it to its original luster. The end result, we believe, is not a "new and improved" version of Cuyler's work filtered by Van Neste and Wainscott. Rather, it is the original version revived and restored for a new audience.

That means there are references you will read that may seem to lack relevance for twenty-first century pastors (i.e., Temperance societies, Young People's Associations, Sabbath Schools). But we encourage you to recognize that while the specific circumstances, names, and/or methods may have changed since 1890, the general principles that Cuyler calls for are still very applicable today. So, do not dismiss his wisdom simply because he speaks from a different era. Much has changed, but much about the nature of pastoral ministry remains the same.

CONCLUSION

We both can honestly say that we would have been better pastors, and the congregations we pastored would have been better served, had we read Cuyler's work when we were younger and just beginning in ministry. Our hope for those younger pastors who are just now beginning in ministry (and for seasoned pastors who need these reminders) is that they will read this work, heed its counsel, and put its lessons into practice—for their good and for the good of their congregations. If that happens, then our efforts in reproducing this work will be well rewarded.

Ray Van Neste and Justin Wainscott

Chapter 1

The Importance of Pastoral Labor

A GREAT NUMBER OF volumes have been written on the art of preaching. Lectures on homiletics have been multiplied until they would form a respectable library. But a large part of the labors of every settled minister lies outside of the pulpit. They embrace the whole sphere of his personal intercourse with his flock, his care of the sick and the suffering, his dealings with awakened or doubting or troubled souls, his organization of Christian work, his development of the spiritual life of the church, and his executive oversight of all its manifold activities. Upon this vitally important side of ministerial life the current literature is quite scanty.

Richard Baxter's *Reformed Pastor* is a classic of undisputed value; but it is now more seldom studied than it ought to be, and the circumstances in which modern ministers are placed are very different from those which surrounded the immortal "bishop" of Kidderminster. About forty years ago (in 1850) Dr. Ichabod Smith Spencer,[1] of Brooklyn, issued a very remarkable work entitled *A Pastor's Sketches*, which attracted wide attention and admiration.

---

1. Ichabod Spencer (1798–1854), longtime pastor of Second Presbyterian Church of Brooklyn and renowned pastor and preacher of his era. He was referred to as "the Bunyan of Brooklyn."

It was devoted to a narrative of specific "cases of conscience" and of conversation with anxious inquirers, his dealings with whom exhibited a most surprising sagacity. Other volumes, more or less similar to Dr. Spencer's brilliant book, have been published. There still seems to be, however, a vacant niche for another treatise which shall discuss in the most familiar, colloquial, and practical fashion, the everyday duties of a Christian pastor. At the solicitation of several of my ministerial brethren, I have been led to undertake such a discussion; and if the results of forty-four years of experience and observation shall prove to be of value to others—especially to my younger brethren—I shall be thankful.

The importance of all that portion of a minister's work that lies *outside of his pulpit* can hardly be overestimated. What is the chief object of the Christian ministry? It goes without saying that it is to win souls to Jesus Christ. A great element of power with every faithful ambassador of Christ should be heart-power. A majority of all congregations, rich or poor, are reached and influenced, not so much through the intellect as through the affections. This is an encouraging fact; for while only one man in ten may have the talent to become a very great preacher, the other nine, if they love Christ and love human souls, can become great pastors. Nothing gives a minister such heart-power as personal acquaintance with, and personal attentions to, those whom he aims to influence; for everybody loves to be noticed. Especially is personal sympathy welcome in seasons of trial. Let a pastor make himself at home in everybody's home; let him come often and visit their sick rooms, and kneel beside their empty cribs, and their broken hearts, and pray with them; let him go to the businessmen in his congregation when they have suffered reverses and give them a word of cheer; let him be quick to recognize the poor and the children, and he will weave a cord around the hearts of his people that will stand a prodigious pressure. His inferior sermons (for every minister is guilty of such occasionally) will be kindly condoned, and he can launch the most pungent truths at his auditors and they will not take offense. He will have won their hearts to himself, and that is a great step towards drawing them to the house of God and winning their souls to the Savior. "A house-going minister," said Chalmers,[2] "makes a church-going people."

Never must the chief end of a minister's labors be lost sight of. It is to awaken the careless, to warn the endangered, to comfort the sorrowing, to help the weak, and to edify believers; in short, to make bad people good and good people better. Preaching strong, gospel sermons is one of the most effective means to this end, but it is not the only means. Outside of the pulpit every messenger of Christ can come to close quarters with each individual soul and preach eye to eye; nobody can dodge such preaching or fall to sleep under it. If the shepherd can only save the sheep by going after the sheep, then woe be unto him if he neglect his duty! As many souls are won to Jesus Christ outside of the pulpit as in the pulpit. I am firmly persuaded that if many a minister would take part of the time that he now spends in polishing his discourses or in miscellaneous studies and would devote it to pastoral visitation, he would have larger congregations and a far larger number of conversions to Christ. He would be a healthier man for the physical exercise of going from house to house; he would be a more fluent speaker from the practice he would gain in personal conversation; and he would become a much more tender, eloquent, and heart-moving ambassador of his Master.

There is one potent argument for close pastoral intercourse with his congregation that many ministers are in danger of ignoring or of underestimating. Every pulpit needs to be vitalized by close contact with living people rather than with lifeless books; and the best practical discourses are those which the congregation help their minister to prepare. His books teach him many truths in the abstract; his people can teach him those and many more truths in the concrete. By constant and loving intercourse with the individuals of his flock, he becomes acquainted with their peculiarities, and thus enlarges his knowledge of human nature, which is second only to a knowledge of God's Word. He discovers also their spiritual wants. He soon becomes convinced that they care

2. Thomas Chalmers (1780–1847), Scottish minister and leader in the Free Church of Scotland.

most to have clear, strong, practical instruction about their everyday duties, trials, and temptations. They want to know not only
how to save their souls for eternity, but how to save their lives in
this world. They want portable truth that they can carry with them
into their homes, into their sick rooms, into their stores and shops,
and into every nook and corner of daily life. If a minister is a wise
man (and neither God nor man has any use for fools), he will be
made all the wiser by the thousand suggestions which he can gain
from the immortal beings to whom he preaches.

There is about as much human nature in the pulpit as there is
in the pew. We all love honest commendation and encouragement.
Nothing cheers and helps a pastor more than to have his people say
to him during the week, "I thank you for last Sunday's sermon; it
did me solid good; it relieved some of my doubts, it lifted off some
of my loads, it comforted me under my heartaches, it brought me
nearer to Christ." Such encouragements not only reveal to us what
our people need, but they are a hundredfold better "pay" than a
salary. A very distinguished and evangelical minister once said to
me rather sadly, "I don't get that sort of encouragement once in six
months." Probably the real reason is that he spends so much of his
time in his study, preparing his superb sermons, that he does not
go familiarly among his flock and give them a chance to say such
cheering and helpful things. They listen to him, love him, and are
proud of him, but are not enough "in touch" with him. And when
I have read his masterly discourses, I have often thought that their
only lack was the lack of just those tender, close, comforting home-
truths which an intimate, personal intercourse with his people
would suggest to him. He is a very great preacher, but perhaps
would be still greater if he were a pastor-preacher.

In Dundee, I conversed with a gray-headed member of St. Peter's Presbyterian Church, who, in his youth, listened to the sainted
Robert Murray McCheyne. He spoke of him with the deepest rev-
erence and love. But the chief thing that he remembered—after
forty-six years—was that McCheyne, a few days before his death,
met him in the street, and laying his hand on his shoulder, said to
him, kindly, "Jimmy, I hope that all is well with your soul. How is

your sick sister? I am coming to see her again shortly." That sentence or two had stuck to the old Christian for over forty years. It had grappled his pastor to him. And this little narrative gave me a fresh insight into the secret of McCheyne's wonderful power. He was a man of rare spirituality and knowledge of God's Word; he was a tender, soul-awakening minister of Jesus Christ; his ministry was richly successful; and largely because he kept in touch with his people and was a pastor as well as a powerful preacher.

Ought every minister to strive to be popular? Yes, if that word be used in its legitimate sense. Of course, the mere hunger for applause from selfish motives is an utter degradation of a high and holy calling. Such unsanctified ambition is a cancer that gnaws away the vitals of every man who falls prey to it. But there is a laudable desire of popularity. Every herald of God's Word should strive to "commend himself to every man's conscience in the sight of God" (2 Cor 4:2) and to "let no man despise him" (1 Tim 4:12). We are told that the common people (i.e., the mass of the people irrespective of social caste) heard Jesus Christ gladly.

To gain the ear and to win the affection of our fellow men is as much a part of our duty as it is to study our Bibles. What is the use of studying the Bible if we cannot get people to hear us expound it? The secret of a legitimate and permanent popularity is this: first, keep your heart strong and sweet and loving and courageous by a constant living in Jesus Christ; and secondly, take a personal interest in everybody. To each human being on this globe nobody is quite as important as his own self. This is not egotism or self-conceit; it is an instinct. The poor man who blacks my boots or saws my wood is a more important person to himself than Bismarck[3] or Gladstone.[4] What becomes of the German or the British Empire is of less consequence to that obscure son of toil than that he should earn a dime to buy his breakfast. This instinct is universal. Every ambassador of Christ should avail himself of it and use it. He should endeavor to find out the character, condition,

3. Otto von Bismarck (1815–1898), first chancellor of the German Empire.
4. William Gladstone (1809–1898), British statesman who served for twelve years as Prime Minister of the United Kingdom.

and needs of every person within his reach. He should put himself into personal sympathy with everybody. The man who is called to proclaim the glorious gospel is bound to preach it winsomely as well as boldly—whether his parish be in a rustic region or in the crowded hive of a great city. Popularity is power. Use it for God!

A western clergyman once addressed to me the inquiry whether eastern ministers regard pastoral labors as befitting an intellectual and manly ministry? What the opinion of other "eastern pastors" may be, I cannot affirm; but I have a very decided opinion that the ministry of Paul and his Divine Master were both intellectual and manly. They both devoted a great deal of time and effort to personal interviews, often with very humble individuals. Three of Christ's most memorable and precious utterances were delivered to a single auditor—Nicodemus (John 3:1–21), the Samaritan woman (John 4:1–42), and the rich young ruler (Matt 19:16–30; Mark 10:17–30; Luke 18:18–30). Jesus Christ made a great many pastoral visits. If my western brother means by the word *manly* to describe uncompromising fidelity to conscience in the face of jeers or scoffs, then it is a prime essential in every minister; but it is equally essential that he be *womanly* in sympathetic tenderness and *childlike* in simplicity and meekness. Manliness is a good thing; godliness is still better; imitation of Jesus Christ is best of all.

Perhaps our friend had formed his estimate of pastoral work from the remark of a certain famous preacher that he "had no time to gossip over a cup of tea with old women." That was his plausible excuse for neglecting to visit his people; but he has paid the penalty for it in the fact that while he has attracted a vast crowd around his brilliant and orthodox pulpit, he has not built up a compact, well-organized, moneygiving church. I maintain that the upbuilding and perpetuation of a strong, working church depends quite as much upon close personal oversight as upon popular preaching. In a solid wall each stone must be handled; each has its place; and the soft "pudding stones" must be kept out of places where the heavy strain comes. Faithful pastoral labor is quite a different thing from "gossiping from house to house." It requires brains and patience and consecration to the holy purpose of saving souls. It consumes time; but how can the same time be spent more profitably elsewhere? If any minister of the gospel fancies himself to be too intellectual or too manly to undertake such patient labors for his Master, he has mistaken his calling. He had better take to literature or the lyceum-platform or a chair of philosophy.

It is an encouraging thought that the humblest minister may become a faithful and successful pastor. God never intended that this world should be saved by pulpit geniuses or else He would create more of them. The average Christian must serve this world if it is saved at all. Every herald of the gospel who loves his Master, loves his Bible, loves his fellow men, and who hungers to win souls to the Savior, can be a good pastor, if he honestly aims to become one. The Lord Jesus Christ, in this respect as in every other, is our model. "I am the Good Shepherd; the shepherd knoweth His sheep; He calleth all His sheep by name" (John 10:14).

Chapter 2

Pastoral Visits

I HAVE ALREADY EMPHASIZED the vital importance of establishing a close personal intercourse with all the people among whom you labor. You can do but little good with your sermons to those who dislike you, and no good at all to those who refuse to hear you. The business of a minister of Christ is not simply to preach the Word, but to win hearers to the Word; still more, to win them to become doers of the Word. Congregations are built up externally by thorough pastoral work, and then they are built up internally by a thorough setting forth of Bible truth. It is one thing to attract a gaping crowd to witness a display of pulpit pyrotechny; it is quite another thing to attract and to hold attentive listeners to the gospel of life. When I was a lad upon a sheep farm, I had to gather the flock to the troughs before they could be fed, and I found it a good plan to go out among them with a basket of oats on my arm.

Set it down as a prime rule to spend part of every day in circulating among your people. Do not let your library—no, not even your Bible or your sermon study—entice you away from your pastoral duties. If your mornings are spent in honest study, you can devote the after-part of the day to itinerating. If you go in the right way to a man's house, you are very likely to win him and to hold him in God's house. "The sermon always sounds better to me on Sunday when I have had a shake of my minister's hand during the week." This was the very natural remark of a very sensible parishioner. The invitations and instructions of God's Word come with tenfold more power from one whom we love than from the man who treats us with indifference and neglect.

After all, the chief power of a Christian minister is *heart-power*. That is Christ's real power over you and me. The pride of a congregation may be awakened by brilliant pulpit displays, but it is personal attention and affectionate sympathy with each individual that bind our congregations to us with hooks of steel. And when we have grappled the affections of our people to us, they will bear any amount of close, searching truth and of the most pungent rebukes of their personal sins, without flinching. I once opened a pulpit-broadside against a certain sin which would inevitably have driven a certain pewholder outside of the doors, if I had not previously got a strong hold on him by pastoral attention in a time of trouble. Conscience often requires a "plainspoken" minister of God to put a severe strain on the tether that binds him to his pastorate; at such times it is a happy thing for him if that tether is securely fastened to a hundred or more family altars and firesides. Some brethren make a sad mistake when they imagine that they lost their situations because they preached the truth too faithfully, or because their people would not endure sound doctrine. Perhaps the real cause was that they had been poor pastors and never had acquired any genuine grip on the personal affection of their flocks. Not one minister in ten is ever dismissed on account of his fidelity to any duty.

Of course, if you are a faithful pastor, you will secure a regular visit to every family in your flock once (or more often) in every year. But extra emergencies demand an extra call promptly. Sudden affliction demands an immediate visit. If you are a sagacious "watchman" (Ezek 33:7–9), you will also be very prompt in giving attention to any case of difficulty or disaffection. For example, Mr. A— has become very sore on account of some scandal raised against him, or on account of his pew rent, or from some imagined unkindness on your part. Human nature gets sore on any spot that is sensitive. Whenever you learn of any such case, put on your hat at the earliest practicable moment, and go straightway to that man, and have a frank, honest talk with him. In a few minutes you may prevent that sore from festering or may heal it on the spot. Perhaps the man has been injured, and you may redress his injury; he will love you ever afterward. Perhaps he was quite in the wrong, and then you have an opportunity to point out his error and to do him good. Do not be afraid to deal honestly with him. The probe or the lancet kindly used may save him from worse things to follow. Nathan did the best job of his life when he dealt faithfully with a very prominent transgressor (2 Sam 12:1–15).

These prompt dealings with offended people or with "crotchety" people or with backsliders and wrongdoers are not the pleasant part of a pastor's work; they are not half so agreeable as attending weddings or visiting warm-hearted, stimulating disciples of Christ. But you are not fit for your sacred office if you shirk any duty because it is disagreeable. It goes against the grain to call upon certain persons, especially to talk plainly with them about their sins or the salvation of their souls. Ah, how often we ministers feel ashamed of ourselves when we find that these very persons were wondering why we did not come to them sooner and interest ourselves in their welfare!

Set it down as a cardinal principle, my young brother, that if you would interest people in the gospel and interest them in their salvation, you have got to interest *yourself* in them and all that belongs to them. You must win them to yourself and win them to the sanctuary, if you would win them to Christ. Find out, therefore, where your people live, and keep a careful record of their residences. Be sure to remember where poor old Mr. A— or blind Mother B— or bedridden Mrs. C— lives, and never let them feel that they are neglected. If a businessman in your parish has met with a sad reverse, go at once to his counting room and give him a warm shake of the hand and a word of encouragement. When you grasp his hand, he will slip the key to his heart into yours. If you learn that the son or daughter in any family has fallen into open disgrace, then is the time for you to pay them a tender visit and give them confidential counsels as well as sympathy. If the tidings of serious sickness reach you from any dwelling, lose no time in getting there. A soul may be very near to eternity and may need your presence most imperatively. The person that wants you is the person that you want. And if you are always on the lookout and always at the post where a service for your Master can be rendered, you will never complain that time hangs heavy on your hands or that "your field is not large enough" for you.

The excuse that is sometimes made that a congregation is *too large* for any man's oversight is absurd. All things are possible to the faithful man who understands the value of time and is a miser of the minutes. Dr. S. H. Tyng, Sr.,[1] was for many years the rector of the largest Episcopal church in New York, and yet he visited every family in his flock. Dr. John Hall,[2] who has at this time the largest Presbyterian parish, and Dr. Wm. M. Taylor,[3] who has the largest Congregational parish, are both systematic pastors; they know the geography of every household committed to their charge. Yet these three men never scrimped their sermon preparations.

I once took occasion to say that there is about one minister (or two) in every generation who is so situated that he cannot be a visitant of his vast flock. Charles H. Spurgeon is that man in the present generation. With a membership of four thousand souls— with the charge of a theological school, a religious magazine, and a dozen missions of charity (and tormenting twinges of the gout besides)—he cannot be expected to visit eight or nine hundred families. He leaves pastoral duties to his brother and his Board of Elders. When Mr. Spurgeon does meet his parishioners, he is very approachable and affable.

1. Stephen H. Tyng (1800–1885), leader of the evangelical wing of the Episcopal Church. The church referred to above is St. George's Episcopal, where Tyng pastored for over three decades.

2. John Hall (1829–1898), longtime pastor of Fifth Avenue Presbyterian Church in New York.

3. William Taylor (1829–1895), after years of fruitful ministry in Scotland and England, pastored Broadway Tabernacle in New York for twenty years.

Pastoral work is a thing to be learned by practice, just like making a hat or conducting a lawsuit. Books will not help you much, but a genuine heart-love for Christ, and a personal sympathy with human souls, will make you successful. (If you do not possess these two essentials, you have mistaken your calling and had better get out of the ministry.) As soon as you take charge of a church whose call you have accepted, begin your tour of visitation at once. Do not omit a single house occupied by anyone who either attends your church regularly or occasionally. In order to ascertain their whereabouts, make an urgent request from the pulpit for every family (or single person) to furnish you their residence. Also, from time-to-time request all those who have changed their residences to inform you promptly of the fact. I often urge my people to inform me promptly of every case of serious sickness. The neglect to do this sometimes involves serious mischief. I never accept as an excuse for this neglect the remark, "You ought to have *missed* me from church and come to inquire after me." It is not a minister's business to take the census of his congregation every Sabbath; and a person may be absent from a dozen causes. Ministers are not omniscient; and we must press upon our people the necessity of keeping us constantly informed as to *everything* in their households which we ought to know—whether it be a case of sickness, or of peculiar affliction, or of a soul awakened to a conviction of sin. Whatever touches your people's hearts should touch yours. You cannot keep the tie between pastor and flock too close or too strong.

I have seldom found it wise to send word in advance to families in my parish that I would visit them on a certain day or hour. For I might be prevented from coming, and thus subject them to disappointment and annoyance. Unless you are sent for to visit a particular house for a particular purpose, it is the best plan to arrange each day's visitations to suit yourself. If you come in upon your people unawares (as you commonly will), it depends very much upon yourself whether you are cordially welcomed. If you enter the house with a hearty salutation and a kind word—without a chilling or stately reserve—and if you tell them to "allow you to sit down among them as they are," without their running off to "dress," or without subjecting you to formal frigidities of the parlor, you will soon be perfectly at home with them.

When you get into frank, friendly conversation with them, do your best to *draw them out*. Encourage them to talk about the Sabbath services, the truths preached, the difficulties raised or allayed, the light afforded, or the comforts given. Encourage them to speak of any special effects of the Word upon any of themselves. In this way you discover whether you are really interesting your auditors, whether you are making yourself understood, and whether your heavenly messages are producing spiritual results. Fishing for compliments is too contemptible to deserve even a rebuke; but it does cheer a minister's heart to be told: "Your sermon has helped me all this week;" or, "Your discourse cleared up a difficult passage for me;" or, "I made up my mind last Sunday that I will try to serve God." Nothing delights me so much as to have a child talk to me about my sermons; for I have tried to adhere to a fixed rule—*never* to deliver a discourse which did not contain at least something in it which would attract and take hold of every average child in the house. Why is it that so many ministers of Christ forget Christ's own example in making truth simple, picturesque, and intelligible to the young and the ignorant?

When calling on your parishioners, frown down all attempts at gossip, and seal your ears against malicious scandal. If one person has a charge against a fellow member, and you see that an enmity may be engendered, you may win the benedictions pronounced on "the peacemaker" by your good offices and so prevent a pimple from becoming a festering sore. The true time to take hold of a quarrel is in its first stages. Of course, if the way opens, you will pray with the families you visit; but they will commonly wait for you to offer to do so.

If anyone in the house asks or needs a personal conversation about his or her soul's welfare, by all means, endeavor that it be private. The timid will never unlock their heart-troubles in the presence of others. Sometimes a case will occur which will require several visits and much probing conversation. Do not begrudge the time. To save one soul is joy enough for an angel; and there is no school in practical theology like dealing with a soul in its struggles and temptations. I hope you will study thoroughly Dr. Spencer's unrivaled *Pastor's Sketches*. He was the Bunyan of Brooklyn; the secret of his success was that he always aimed to cooperate with the Holy Spirit.

When in your pastoral rounds, you will sometimes have the opportunity to do more execution in a single talk than in a hundred sermons. I once spent an evening in a vain endeavor to bring a man to a decision for Christ. Before I left he took me upstairs to the nursery to show me his beautiful children in their cribs. I said to him tenderly: "Do you mean that these sweet children shall never have any help from their father to get to heaven?" He was deeply moved, and in a month became an active member of my church. For twenty-five years that man has been glued to me; infinitely better, he has steadily glorified his Savior.

On a cold winter evening I made my first call on a rich merchant in New York. As I left his door, and the piercing gale swept in, I said, "What an awful night for the poor!" He went back, and bringing to me a roll of bank bills, he said, "Please hand these, for me, to the poorest people you know." After a few days I wrote to him the grateful thanks of the poor whom his bounty had relieved, and added: "How is it that a man who is so kind to his fellow creatures has always been so unkind to his Savior as to refuse Him his heart?" That sentence touched him in the core. He sent for me to come and talk with him, and speedily gave himself to Christ. He has been a most useful Christian ever since. But he told me that I was the first person who had talked to him about his soul in nearly twenty years! One hour of pastoral work did more for that man than the pulpit efforts of a lifetime.

Chapter 3

Visitation of the Sick and Funeral Services

IT IS A DUTY which every family in your congregation owes to their pastor, as well as to themselves, that they should inform you promptly of every case of serious sickness. Nor can you be too prompt in responding to such a call. However busy you may be in preparing a sermon or in any commendable occupation, everything else must be laid aside; a pastor should be as quick to hasten to the room of sickness as an ambulance is to reach a scene of disaster. You may find that your parishioner has been suddenly attacked with dangerous illness and that even your entrance into the sick room may be agitating to the patient; at such times you will need to use all the tact and delicacy and discretion that you can command. Do not needlessly endanger a sick body by your efforts to guide or to console the immortal spirit that may be hovering on the brink of the eternal world. Let your words be few, calm, tender, and every syllable you speak *point towards Jesus*. Whoever the sufferer may be—saint or sinner—his failing vision should be directed to "no man save Jesus only" (Matt 17:8). Let the prayer also which you offer be brief, and in the tenderest language in which

15

you can breathe out a fervid supplication to the God of all grace. It is not commonly the office of a pastor to tell a patient that his or her disease is assuredly a fatal one; but if you know that death is near, then in the name of the Master, be faithful as well as tender.

There are many cases of extreme and critical illness, when the presence of even the most loving pastor may be an unwise intrusion. An excellent Christian lady who had been twice apparently at the brink of death said to me, "Never enter the room of a person who is extremely low, unless the person urgently requests you, or unless a spiritual necessity compels it. You have no idea how the sight of a new face agitates the sufferer, or how you may unconsciously and unintentionally rob that sufferer of some of the little life that is fluttering in that feeble frame." I felt grateful to the good woman for her advice and have often acted upon it accordingly when the family have unwisely importuned me to do what would be of more harm than benefit. On some occasions when I have found a sick room crowded by well-meaning but needless intruders, I have taken the liberty to "put them all forth" as our Master did from that chamber in which the daughter of Jairus was in the death slumber (Matt 9:18–26; Mark 5:21–43; Luke 8:40–56).

A large portion of the time and attention which you bestow upon the sick will be demanded by chronic sufferers who have been confined to their beds of weariness for many months or years. Whoever you may neglect, do not neglect them. Visit them as often as possible. Bring into their rooms the sunshine of a cheerful countenance and a morsel of fresh manna from heaven that shall have the taste of honey. Some of those bedridden sufferers are "prisoners of Jesus Christ," who can do you quite as much good as you can do for them. What eloquent sermons they can preach to you on the beauty of submissive patience and on the supporting power of the Everlasting Arm! Such interviews strengthen your own faith, soften your own heart, and infuse into it the spirit of Him who "took our infirmities and bore our sickness" (Isa 53:4; Matt 8:14–17). McCheyne of Dundee said that before preaching on the Sabbath he sometimes visited some parishioner who might be lying extremely low, for he found it good "to take a look *over the verge*."

Visitation of the Sick and Funeral Services

The hour you spend in the abodes of sickness and of sorrow will often subject your nerves and your sympathetic sensibilities to a pretty severe strain, and from such trials you must not shrink. But the most difficult and delicate part of your pastoral duties will be the conducting of funeral services. At such trying services too many ministers sadly fail; some from want of sense and some from want of sensibility. The first class offend by their unwise utterances; the second offend by their utter lack of sympathy; to them a funeral is as "professional" an affair as it is to the undertaker.

In making the arrangements for funeral services, the first persons to be consulted are the bereaved family; their wishes must be respected. Unless in a few and rare cases where public honors are to be paid to public men, the last services will be of a domestic character; and the simpler they are the better. I always love to see the kindred occupy the same apartment in which the form of the beloved one lies sleeping; it seems far more affectionate to sit beside their dead than to leave a parent, a wife, or a child to be surrounded by chance-gathered neighbors or strangers. The pastor should also, if possible, stand close beside the mourning family and not be thrust away into another part of the dwelling. We are often stationed upon a stairway in the hall, with nothing to look at but a blank wall or the heads of the people congregated below us. This detracts from the naturalness of the service, and puts us, as it were, out of sympathy with those whom we desire to comfort. We are affected through the eye, and the sight of the slumbering dead and the sorrowing kindred is apt to stir the fount of feeling in our own hearts. Cold formality is the unpardonable sin in the house of mourning. No matter what suffering it may cost us, or however severe may be the strain upon our nerves, we pastors must not shirk the suffering. It is no place to harden the heart or to retreat into a frigid formality. A funeral is a heart-service; let your own heart have its way. The closer you follow your own best instincts, the fewer blunders will you commit. Put yourself in the place of the mourner, and then speak as your feelings dictate.

So far have I aimed to carry out this principle that I rarely prepare any funeral address. I store my mind with the chief facts and circumstances of the occasion and then allow the heart to utter its own words of sympathy and consolation. Set speeches beside a coffin are icicles. Stale truisms about death are often a solemn impertinence. Elaborate addresses are usually as much out of place as at a communion table. Simplicity and tenderness are the prime essentials. Grief is always simple, and bleeding hearts must be touched tenderly. Honest eulogy of those who have lived nobly and for God's glory is often a duty to the living as well as a deserved tribute to the one who has fallen asleep in Jesus. The instincts of a minister's heart ought to tell him how much to say; but let him not disown or dishonor the grace of God that dwelt in the life just ended. The last experiences of the last hours of the departed are sometimes full of eloquent inspirations, and we ought to rehearse them to cheer the faith of the survivors. A sudden death is in itself a tremendous sermon; and we may enforce the solemn lesson if we do it discreetly and lovingly. Grant that but few persons have ever been converted by funeral addresses; we should nonetheless speak in the same direction that the Almighty God is speaking. While comforting the bereaved we may incidentally gain a strong hold on some unconverted souls, and thus the way be opened to lead them to Christ.

No funeral service is adequate or proper in which there is not a large use of appropriate Scripture and also the singing of one or more hymns. Sometimes an elaborate musical performance is provided that would better befit a concert room. Nothing goes quite so close to the heart as the tender and tearful singing of some sweet hymn like "Rock of Ages," or "Jesus, Lover of My Soul," or "Abide with Me," or "Asleep in Jesus." A hymn sinks deeper into the soul than a discourse. Tears are a blessed escape valve for pent-up, overpowering grief, and the more freely they are evoked during the last services of affection, the greater will be the relief to suffering hearts. Pray that God may make you a "son of consolation" (Acts 4:36) while you are standing between the living and the dead. Yet your office as a comforter does not end when the silent form has been committed to the bosom of mother-earth. The hardest strain upon the bereaved will come when the obsequies are all over and the crowd has gone, and the sorrowing ones come back to the empty house and home and hearts. Then you will be needed most, and then will it be your office to guide the trembling hands and point the weeping eyes to that Friend that sticketh closer than a brother. May the dear Master give you grace to speak a "word in season to them that are weary" (Isa 50:4) and to lift many a sobbing, suffering soul up into the sweet sunshine that streams from the heavenly throne!

Chapter 4

The Treatment of the Troubled

A LARGE PART OF every Christian minister's work must be given to those who are in trouble. The careless are to be awakened by faithful, pungent proclamation of the sinfulness of sin and the certainty of its endless retribution; the inquirers are to be directed, and God's people to be fed with their rations of solid food. But every week brings before his pulpit, or under his eye in pastoral visitation, some of that numerous class who need a lift or a helping hand. Bruised hearts are to be bound up; feeble knees to be strengthened; a word in season to be spoken to the weary or the weak or the woebegone. Tonic sermons are always in order, the stronger the better; some of our flock get terribly run down by Saturday night and need fresh infusion of iron in the blood. There are two sorts of trouble that demand kind, careful, and wise treatment.

∾

(1) The first sort belongs to those who are in the fold of Christ. All true Christians are not happy Christians. While "Great Heart" and "Hopeful" go striding and singing on their way to the Celestial City, poor Mr. Despondency and Mr. Littlefaith and Sister Much-afraid hobble along painfully and need a helping hand

pretty often.[1] It takes all sorts of Christians to make an average church. Some are constitutionally despondent about everything. It is not easy to change natural temperament; let such travel the straight road conscientiously, even if their heads often droop like the bulrush; they will find heaven's sunshine and song all the more welcome when they get there. Uneasy as this kind of Christian often is about himself, he seldom gives much uneasiness to his pastor. It is the self-confident, dash-ahead professor that we are often anxious about. Another class owe their despondency to ill health. The flesh and the spirit lie mighty close together, and they act and react upon each other. That ripe old saint, Dr. Archibald Alexander,[2] suffered from such a peculiar nervous disorder that he was always gloomy when an east wind blew. Dyspepsia[3] puts some of Christ's choice ones into the dumps; a dose of medicine or a bottle of Saratoga water[4] will bring more relief than a prayer or a Bible text. The saddest case of religious despair I ever encountered came from physical disease, and the lady was shocked when I told her so. Yet as soon as the torpid liver was set right, her soul was filled with light and gladness.

But the most frequent cases that the pastor has to deal with are those who are suffering under some trying dispensation of Providence. Disappointment has shattered their schemes, or pecuniary adversities have crippled them, or death has smitten the four corners of their house, and their hearts are breaking. To try to stanch the tears of persons who are in deep grief is a folly, even if it were possible. Tears are the safety valve of grief, and often keep an agonized heart from bursting; let them flow. When nature has had her way, grace may begin to work. In dealing with the afflicted—from whatever cause it come—we must treat them always as scholars in God's school of suffering. The temptation of the devil to

---

1. References all taken from John Bunyan, *The Pilgrim's Progress*.

2. Archibald Alexander (1772–1851), first professor at Princeton Theological Seminary, where he served for almost four decades.

3. Dyspepsia is more commonly known as indigestion.

4. The waters of Saratoga Springs (in New York) were revered as a natural source of health and rejuvenation.

such sufferers is to get them into a quarrel with God; if he cannot do that, he tries to break their lanterns and leave them in the dark. As long as a Christian's anchor holds, he can ride out any hurricane of trouble; but if his cable that fastens him to Christ is cut, he goes helplessly on the rocks.

The true way to look at affliction is as a prime part of a Christian's education. The only relief I have ever found myself when under sharp bereavement was in the heaven ordered certainty that this world is only a preparatory school for the better and the endless life beyond. Terribly hard lessons in "division" and "subtraction" are often assigned us; we are put on the back benches and the lowest, when we fancy ourselves entitled to the highest. Our textbooks are often stained with tears, and our loving Teacher often uses the rod. The strongest Christians are made by a costly education. The very word *disciple* signifies a little learner, and the chief object of all discipline is to develop character. The core of Christianity is obedience to our Divine Master, and the highest attainment is to let him have His own way. Often when the hard lesson starts the tears and makes the heart ache, the blessed Teacher comes close and whispers in our ears, "As many as I love I chasten; no chastening for the present seemeth to be joyous, but grievous; nevertheless afterward it yieldeth the peaceable fruit of righteousness" (Rev 3:19; Heb 12:11). It is the "afterward" that vindicates God's dealings. Noble old Richard Baxter exclaimed after a life of severe toil and suffering, "God, I thank thee for a bodily discipline of eight and fifty years!" Out of the school of trial the Master brings his ripest, holiest pupils. The best pruned vines yield the richest clusters; the brightest gold comes out of the hottest furnace. A glorious promotion will it be—when the life-school is over—that they whose hearts have ached and whose eyes have so often wept, will be graduated into the magnificent inheritance of the Father's house!

Two things are chiefly to be aimed at in the treatment of desponding or bereaved Christians. The first is to get them out of themselves, and the other is to get them into active service for their Master. The tides of inward feeling are in danger of stagnating into a fen of bitter waters. Sluice them off, and turn them into streams of beneficence to others. A sorely bereaved lady once said to me, "If I could not keep my mind occupied in Christian labor for the poor and elsewhere, I should go crazy with grief." Useful occupation is both a tonic to faith and a sedative to sorrow. If troubles drive us to toils for our Master, then the useful toils will in turn, drive away many of the troubles.

∾

(2) There is a second sort of troubles to be dealt with which belong to those who are outside of Christ's fold and who find obstacles in the way of their getting in. They are plagued with doubts and unbelief. A careful discrimination must be made between the willful skeptics who will not believe, and the involuntary ones who find it hard to believe. This latter class merit the kindest and most gentle treatment, such as Jesus showed to the father of the demoniac child (Matt 17:14–19; Mark 9:14–29; Luke 9:37–43) and to doubting Thomas (John 20:24–29). We should aim to discover just what it is that they find it difficult to believe. Are they puzzled and perplexed with such mysteries as the nature of the Trinity, or the doctrine of election, or the existence of sin in the world, or any other hard nut that human ingenuity cannot crack? Let all such mysteries alone; they are an overmatch for the mightiest brains ever created; the secret things belong unto God. Happily, our salvation does not depend on unlocking mysteries.

"I find it hard to believe in Christ," says the troubled inquirer, when he is pushed to the sticking point. "Have you ever honestly tried to do it in the way that Christ commands?" That is the query which we should press on such a person. Saving faith in Christ is not an abstract opinion; it is an act; it is putting yourself into connection with the Savior. Have you with empty hand grasped hold on Him in honest prayer? Have you tried sincerely to follow Him by taking a single step to please Him? Have you endeavored to keep a solitary commandment? Have you, in short, ever obeyed Him? If not, then you must die a doubter; for the only way to be saved by the Lord Jesus is to do what He commands.

To get a troubled sinner out of the region of theory into the region of practice, out of doctrines into duties, is a prime point gained. No one is ever troubled about believing in Christ as soon as he begins to obey Christ. Knowing comes by doing. The loving Savior's hand is immediately stretched out to save everyone who leaps overboard from the boat of sin and struggles toward Him. Unbelief stays in the boat and goes down; faith leaps out and trusts. As Spurgeon pithily says, "The way to do a thing is—to do it."

Chapter 5

How to Have a Working Church

THE PULPIT SERVICES OF a minister occupy only a few hours on each Sabbath; his duties as a pastor extend over all the other days of the week. He may be a very eloquent pulpiteer and yet have an inactive church. Of some plain preachers it may be said as Dr. James W. Alexander[1] once said to me of that noble and admirable pastor, Dr. Asa D. Smith: "I envy Doctor Smith more than any pastor in New York, for he has the art of setting all his people to work, and of keeping them at it."[2] That is a great art; how is it to be acquired? A few suggestions that I have gathered during forty years or more may be of value to beginners in the ministry.

ॐ

(1) If you expect to have an active church, you must be a wide-awake, industrious man yourself. An indolent pastor is apt to

1. James Alexander (1804–1859), son of Archibald Alexander, and served as a professor and a pastor. He was pastor for eight years at Fifth Avenue Presbyterian Church in New York.

2. Asa Smith (1804–1877), longtime pastor of Fourteenth Street Presbyterian Church in New York before becoming the seventh president of Dartmouth College.

have an indolent congregation. If you are found smoking on your lounge or dawdling away your time over light literature; if you are seen oftener out driving for pleasure or sauntering in bookstores and picture galleries, than you are in visiting your flock, then your people will soon hold you cheap and rightly conclude that they have a lazy minister. They will come to the same conclusion if you are ready to put into your pulpit any man who comes along in a clerical coat. Never cheapen your own pulpit. Go to it as often as possible, even if through unavoidable circumstances, you have been prevented from preparing a "finished discourse." An imperfect sermon, if well saturated with prayer and sent home with fervor, may do good execution. Veteran pastors will testify that often the discourses from which they had expected the least, have accomplished the most.

Recreate mind and body with easy occupations on Monday. Get at your sermon on Tuesday—the minister's best day—and never commit the idiotic sin of writing a sermon on Saturday evening. Make the utmost of those hours when your mind works like a trip-hammer and then put upon paper your best thoughts—whether you ever carry the paper into the pulpit or not. Use the forenoons for study, your afternoons for pastoral visitation, and your evenings for meetings or for reading, recreation, or social purposes. Sleep as soundly as possible all night if you want to keep your congregation awake on Sunday. The Irishman's rule for good sleeping was "to pay attention to it."

The men who live the longest, and do the most effective work, are commonly good sleepers. If they cannot secure enough at night, they make it up during the day. When a man who has so much strain on his brain and his sensibilities as a pastor has, goes to his bedroom, he should school himself to the habit of dismissing all thoughts about outside matters. If this cost him some difficulty, he should pray for Divine help to do it. Too many ministers toil at their sermons until eleven or twelve o'clock, and then retire with throbbing heads to their sleepless beds. The man who invented "midnight oil" deserves a purgatory of endless nightmare.

My own rule is never to touch a sermon by lamplight. One hour in the morning is worth five at night.

I have already exhorted you to learn the geography of your parish thoroughly, and to keep yourself in daily intercourse with your people. Do not have any "running places" or favorite resorts; and don't let anybody in the congregation own you. While making your pastoral visits, show an interest in what your people are doing, and then repay yourself by making them interested in what you are doing. Discuss freely the affairs of the church with all your families; commend those who are most prompt at the devotional meetings, and most alert in serving the Master; and kindly chide the delinquents. Let them know that you miss them. A shepherd's "crook" must often be used with the stragglers.

❧

(2) However active you may be, it is vitally important that you should develop the activities of your church members and direct them into fields of usefulness. There is a vast amount of latent power in most of our congregations; and in large churches there is a tendency to say, "Oh, you have enough to do the work without me." As small farms are usually the best tilled, so small churches are often the best worked. There must be leaders in every church; but don't try to push into prominence conceited people who happen to have large purses or social conspicuousness. The best workers are most often those of humblest social rank; and no man or woman should be prominent unless they have earned their position by consecration to the Master's service. Try to discover what a man is best fitted for, and then set him at it. When a new member comes into your church—either by conversion or transmission from another church—do not let him settle down into a mere "passenger." Endeavor to enlist him at once into some line of usefulness. There will be some conceited and presumptuous folk who thrust themselves into positions for which they have no capacity; but such very soon find their level. I have generally found that ardent, zealous Christians, even when sometimes indiscreet, accomplish a great deal more than the over-prudent, phlegmatic

sort. Good Dr. Brainard[3] used to say, "I whip up the fast horses, for there are plenty that don't pull a pound."

∿

(3) Keep your eye on all the operations of the church; not to do the trustees' work, or the elders' work, or the Sunday School superintendent's work, or the class leader's work, but to see that they do it. A meddlesome minister may be as mischievous as an idle one; yet oversight and wise counsel are your prerogative. Always attend your prayer meetings, both for your own spiritual profit and also to put honor on the most vital service, next to the preaching of the Word. As long as you have competent laymen who can lead the meeting, commit the leadership of the service to them; this will develop them, and relieve you of "over much speaking" (Matt 6:7–8). Ministers may talk too often; and if a pastor is especially gifted, there is danger that the church may become a one-man, power machine. Mr. Beecher[4] used to complain that his people were too slow to take part in his prayer meetings; and one cause of this was that he took so large a part in them himself. No church can ever be strong unless the strain is put on their own sinews; there is a place for the Aquilas and Priscillas, as well as for Paul. A timely word from the pastor may help a prayer meeting, but it is the people's service, not his.

∿

(4) As the bottle is the chronic curse of every community, the church of God cannot ignore it. Every minister ought to preach and practice entire abstinence from the intoxicating cup; and every Christian church ought to have a Temperance wheel in its machinery.[5] Therefore, it is wise to organize a society which shall

---

3. It is unclear who Cuyler refers to here as "Good Dr. Brainard."

4. Lyman Beecher (1775–1863), prominent Presbyterian pastor considered by many as one of the most respected religious voices of his era.

5. Cuyler served during a time when the temperance movement was quite prominent. Therefore, such a strong exhortation toward that end would not have been unusual or out of place for Protestant pastors in his day.

not be a political or partisan "annex," but a part of the religious movement of your church, under the supervision of the pastor. The title to membership should be the avowed practice of total abstinence from all intoxicants; and I still believe in the expediency of signing a pledge to thus abstain. A brief constitution, an efficient president, and board of managers, a package of pledges and a good committee to secure proper speakers are the main requisites for such a society. The public meetings should be free; and a collection taken up will meet the current expenses. Such an organization has been a source of social and spiritual blessings in my own and in many other congregations.

∾

(5) Drive every wheel in your machinery to its utmost power, but don't have more wheels than power. Widen your activities as fast as you have men and money to propel them. Organize your young people into an association, with a weekly meeting for prayer and training in Christian work. Organize your women into missionary societies and other benevolent labors. Do not overwork any one department to the sacrifice of others or run your own hobbies to death. Feed your people with the solid meat of the Word, if you want them to be strong for work; and then fire them by constantly pointing them to Jesus and praying for the baptism of the Holy Spirit. Keep Christ in the foreground. Come to your flock every Sabbath with Jesus in your heart and Jesus on your tongue. The only permanent power that can propel any church is the power from on high; and that church which is mighty in prayer is the one that is always mighty in work.

Chapter 6

Training Converts

A VERY LARGE PROPORTION of members in our churches count for very little except upon the muster roll.[1] When that roll is called for practical service, they do not answer, "Here!" The lamentable statistics of contributions show how small are the pecuniary gifts of those comatose Christians. The thin attendance at prayer meetings in too many churches, the fewness of those who take part in them, or in any kind of personal effort for souls and the spread of Christ's kingdom, are illustrations of the same fact. A large portion of the power in the church is a latent power. The stream is diverted upon the water wheels of the world, or else runs to waste; less than half of it turned upon spiritual machinery. One reason, among many, is that new converts are not trained into Christian activity from the start.

Many converts to Christ are still in the morning of life, although they may have outgrown the Sunday School. Under thirty years of age the habits of individuals are easily molded; and during the thirty years after that, they ought to be set to work for their

---

1. The term "muster" refers to the process of accounting for soldiers in the military. The officer in charge of roll call uses a list of names to record who is present, and that list is known as the "muster roll."

Master. The true time to enlist a Christian in active service is when he enlists in the visible army of Christ by a public confession of Christ. If a new convert does not open his lips in some devotional meeting during the first thirty days, he is apt to remain tongue-tied for life. If he or she is not called into some sort of service, then doth he or she become a drone in the hive. One of the most effectual methods that I know of for training new converts is by the agency of a "Young People's Association," organized in the church and under the oversight of the pastor. There has been such an association in the church which I had the honor to serve, for about twenty-five years. Sometimes its membership runs as high as seven hundred.

It embraces three classes of members—active, associate, and honorary. Any member of our church between the ages of fifteen and forty-five may be chosen an "active" member of the association. Any person of good moral character may become an associate member, entitled to all privileges except that of holding office. The fee of membership is fifty cents annually, and ten dollars secures a membership for life. The objects of the Association are to hold weekly devotional meetings, to promote social intercourse, to visit the sick, to search out and bring in young people, to labor for their conversion, and to do whatever will develop the spiritual life of new converts. There is a "Devotional Committee," which has charge of the Monday evening meeting, which is held in the houses of the congregation. This committee must select the house, have it announced from the pulpit, and see to it that the campstools and hymnbooks are taken to the said house in season.

That meeting lasts just one hour. The leader of the service is allowed to occupy fifteen minutes in opening the exercises. As soon as possible after a person is converted, he is requested to take charge of the meeting; this breaks him into the harness at once. No one is allowed to occupy more than three minutes in an address or a prayer. At the close of the service a half hour is spent in giving introductions and in social intercourse. In pleasant weather we expect the house to be crowded; but we have seldom had the spiritual thermometer so high as to pack a house on a stormy evening. Only a pleasure-party or a political caucus can do that.

In these social meetings all are made welcome, and new converts are encouraged to take part. There is a freedom felt in a private house which cannot be felt by a beginner in the public lecture-room of the church. Most persons of modesty and common sense are apt to feel a certain diffidence in speaking or praying for the first time. Some of our most effective speakers made an unpromising start, and had one or two breakdowns before they could, as the oarsmen say, "pull themselves together." But it is not simply a public speaking and praying service into which the Association trains its members. They are organized for various kinds of work. There is a visiting committee to look after the sick. There is an entertainment committee who arrange music, readings, and other pleasant features for a monthly sociable—to which the whole congregation are invited. The monthly entertainments commonly crowd the lecture room or the Sabbath School hall. There is a temperance committee which oversees that branch of Christian labor. Recently a meeting of our young ladies who are interested in this blessed work was very largely attended. For years we had an efficient corps of tract-distributers in the Association; but the removal from town its moving spirits has left this department rather feeble at present. There is also a "relief committee" for cases of poverty, and another one which provides flowers every Sabbath for the pulpit and then sends them to the rooms of the sick.

I have entered more into the details of this Association because it has yielded such precious spiritual fruits. Its graduates are all over the West as active Christians; some of them have entered the gospel ministry. It has been a training school for converts, and as such deserves a place beside the Sabbath School in the affections and prayers of the church. I should almost as soon think of conducting a church without the regular officers as without this educational institution for newborn souls. It helps to solve several such questions as—how to develop the lay element; how to cultivate social intercourse; how to save the young for Christ and keep them out of the clutch of the devil. In the apostolic churches the new material was put to immediate use. That was one reason why the Word grew mightily and prevailed. If the machinery in those days was simpler than now, still there was organized effort, and that was built on personal consecration to Christ. Give us but that, and we shall have few drones in the hive. Conversion without consecration signifies birth without growth—blossoms without fruit.

I have drawn upon my personal observation in this outline of the work done by the Young People's Association of the Lafayette Avenue Church; but the same style of work is being done in many hundreds of churches by the admirable "Societies of Christian Endeavor." Every new convert should enroll himself or herself in such a society if it is within reach. Wherever the circumstances permit I also cordially commend the "Young Men's Christian Association" as a most excellent training school in the service of Christ. There need be no clash or collision between the "Y.M.C.A." and the organization in each individual church.

Chapter 7

Prayer Meetings

THE PRAYER MEETING MAY fairly claim to be regarded as second only to the pulpit in the spiritual life of a Christian church. Some would give it the first place; for while many churches have managed to keep alive without a pastor, none are likely to preserve their vitality and vigor without a regular gathering of the flock for public devotion. Certainly, the prayer meeting is a very fair thermometer; a cold prayer meeting marks a cold church. It is at once the cause, and the effect, of spiritual declension. On the other hand, a well-attended, well-conducted prayer meeting is both a joy to the pastor and a wellspring of blessings to the people. It is preeminently the people's service, and during nearly the whole of my ministry it has been my custom to entrust the charge of the service to the elders, who are the representatives of the congregation. Each elder takes the leadership of the weekly meeting, in alphabetical order. He selects the topic to be discussed and must see to it that the topic is duly announced from the pulpit on the previous Sabbath. For the right management of the meeting he is responsible; and he should make thorough preparation for the solemn charge committed to him.

If there be any religious service that ought to be delivered from frigid formality it is the family gathering of Christ's disciples at the mercy seat. "Cut and dried" addresses are out of place. Long, stereotyped petitions are a weariness to the flesh. A good rule for the pulpit, and an equally good one for the weekly devotional service, is—have something to say, and then say it! Those who come to the service filled with the Spirit are likely to overflow in pithy, inspiring exhortations or in fervent, well-ordered petitions.

It commonly requires the presence of several sensible people to make a good prayer meeting; but it is in the power of one or two weak-headed and troublesome people to mar it most wretchedly. Certain persons of this sort will come into a meeting as moths fly into a candle. They stick there like the moths; but instead of being scorched to death, they nearly extinguish the meeting. Now, it is the imperative duty of the pastor or of the conductor of the service to deal with such brethren most frankly. If self-conceit makes the brother so troublesome, then that self-conceit should be kindly rebuked. If he offends ignorantly, then his ignorance should be kindly corrected. The man who has not enough sense or conscience to take a wise hint gratefully will never be of any value to a devotional meeting. Some good people mar a meeting without intending it. For example, one fluent brother gets to monopolizing the time by the inordinate frequency or the inordinate length of his utterances. I once had an excellent church member who spoke regularly at every prayer service (and it requires a very *full* man to do that profitably). I frankly told him that he was crowding others out of their rights, and also suggested that he might better address the Almighty in petition sometimes instead of always addressing his neighbors in exhortation. He accepted the hint kindly and reformed. Some good speakers would be listened to more eagerly if they relieved their talks with more frequent "flashes of silence."

A prayer meeting is sometimes marred by aimlessness, both in the addresses to the Lord and to each other. Brother A— talks about faith, and Brother B— about the pestilence at Memphis, and Brother C— about . . . no one can exactly tell what; and the prayers go off about as fairly at random as the squibs which boys fire on the

Fourth of July. One method of correcting this aimless diffuseness, and of compacting the service, is to select and announce beforehand some profitable topic for discussion. This may be even selected by the leader and announced on the previous Sabbath. Then everybody has some definite object to aim at in his remarks. Then the whole service hangs together like a fleece of wool, and there is spiritual instruction afforded, as well as a kindling of devotional feeling by a study of God's truth. If a company of Christians will carefully discuss such a practical topic as "Obeying Conscience," or such a passage as the twenty-third psalm, or the parable of the wheat and the tares, they cannot but be instructed and strengthened. Food for devotion will be furnished and both the praying and the speaking will be directed "at a mark." Of course, this arrangement need not hoop a meeting as with iron or forbid anyone from presenting some special request or some matter of immediate interest that lies near his heart. The moment that any system of management kills the freedom of the family gathering at the mercy seat, then the system should be abated. A cast-iron rigidity may be as fatal to the meeting as aimless verbiage. If the Spirit of God is present with great power, there is no danger from either quarter. Wherefore, the most effectual cure for an invalid prayer meeting is to open the lips and the hearts in fervent supplication for the incoming of the Holy Spirit. There may be cases in which a meeting is seriously disturbed by the unwelcome utterances of persons whose character is more than doubtful, and who desire to gain a cheap reputation for piety by taking part in prayer or exhortations. Such transgressors should be frankly informed that they had better remain silent until they are ready to open their lips in honest confession. Mr. Moody[1] pithily says that "a man who pays fifty cents on the dollar when he *could* pay one hundred cents on the dollar had better keep still." To confess flagrant wrongdoing in a social meeting is no easy thing; but I once heard a man do it in a way that not only thrilled the assembly but brought a rich blessing on his own soul and reinstated him in the position which

---

1. Dwight Lyman (D. L.) Moody (1837–1899), famed American evangelist and founder of both Moody Bible Church and Moody Bible Institute.

he had lost. Sincere confession to God or to our fellow men fills a prayer room with an odor as sweet as that of the broken alabaster box in the house of Simon the leper (Matt 26:6–13; Mark 14:3–9). But there is a species of wordy and windy parading of one's own "awful guiltiness," which only nauseates the auditors and cannot impose upon God. It is a terrible thing to tell lies in the name of the Lord. Whatever else be the faults of our prayer services, let them be delivered from pious fraud and solemn falsehood.

Brevity should be rigorously enforced in the prayer meeting, except in those rare cases where an individual is speaking so evidently under the inspiration of the Divine Wisdom that it would be a sin to apply the gag law. Five minutes is commonly long enough for an address and three minutes for a prayer. The model for our petitions, which our Lord has taught us, does not consume half a minute; and even that wonderful intercessory prayer which He offered for His followers on the night of His betrayal occupied just twenty-six sentences. We ministers too often transgress in monopolizing time at our people's devotional meetings. It is *their* meeting. We have ample opportunity for Bible exposition on the Sabbath. If the social meeting has broken down under the weight of long, heavy preachments, it is time it was mended. An energetic leader can do this by a prompt tap of a bell or a kind word of monition, or by calling on some "full" brother to offer a word of prayer. Without dwelling further upon the things which mar the seasons of devotion, I will present briefly in the next chapter an account of a service which fairly realized my ideal of a prayer meeting.

Chapter 8

A Model Prayer Meeting

IT BEGAN PUNCTUALLY AT the moment. As the clock struck eight the leader rose and sounded the *reveille*,[1] by giving out the inspiring lines:

> Come, my soul, thy suit prepare;
> Jesus loves to answer prayer.[2]

A sweet symphony was touched on a piano in one of the crowded rooms, and then the words of the hymn were sent heavenward on a full tide of united and enthusiastic song. Every voice chimed in. Each verse was sung with more spirit than its predecessor, marking the outcome of the rising devotion; and like a strong "offshore" breeze, the opening chant of praise carried the whole meeting out of harbor into the larger liberty and deep waters of the open sea. Then the leader invoked the descent of the Holy Ghost, the gift of utterance, and the Pentecostal baptism. It was a very short prayer, but very full. He prayed for the gift of prayer upon

---

1. A signal to get up. In the military, "to sound reveille" is to give a bugle call at sunrise.

2. The opening lines of the hymn, "Come, My Soul, Thy Suit Prepare," by John Newton.

all, for honesty of speech, for deliverance from dead formalities, for sincerity in confession, for childlike familiarity of approach to God, for filial faith; and then closed by inviting Christ to "come in, as through the closed doors of the disciples' upper room at Jerusalem, and speak, *Peace be unto you*" (John 20:19).

As soon as a fitting passage of the Word had been read, each one present seemed ready to bear his part in giving life and interest to the occasion. Each one felt, "This is not the leader's meeting, nor the pastor's, but *my* meeting with my own spiritual family at the feet of my own Savior. Here I have a right to weep, and sing, and melt in spirit, and flow out in social communings with the brotherhood around me. If I am silent, then the meeting may prove dumb; and if I freeze up then my neighbor may chill through, until the place becomes an ice house." So, there was no entreaty required on the part of the leader to "draw out" those present. He was obliged to use no turnkey. What is more pitiful than to see a poor, embarrassed elder or deacon sit before a petrified company, and after a long, awful pause, in which you can count the clock ticks, beseechingly implore "some brother present to improve the time"? As if the dreary dribble of dullness that was forced out by such a process was not a downright *mis*-improvement and murder of the sweet, sacred hour of devotion. It is no wonder that so many of us grew up with a loathing for the very name, and next to a taste of the birch that grew behind the schoolhouse, we dreaded a sentence to "go to prayer meeting." Our only solace was a sound nap, until someone shook our eyes open, and with an admonitory thump informed us that "meetin's out; it is time to go home."

But even a child of eight years old would have been interested in the enlivening service we are now etching. Not a moment was lost; not a syllable of persuasion was needed. One man rose and gave a touching account of the scene a few evenings before, when he had first set up a family altar in his once prayerless house. That was his first audible prayer, and this was his first speech. While he is speaking, the tears stream down the cheek of his astonished and overjoyed wife. Then comes a fervid prayer of thanksgiving to God from someone present, and a petition that the family altar thus reared may never be desecrated or thrown down. After this a youth arose, with a blue jacket, and an anchor embroidered on his broad collar. He had been brought there by a tract visitor. The burden of his short, artless speech was, come to Jesus. "Whosoever will, let him come," said the sunburnt youth; "that means that everybody on board may come, from the captain to the cabin boy. We are bound for heaven. Christ is our pilot. The anchor is sure and steadfast. Come aboard, friends, before eight bells strike, and your time is up." No one felt like criticizing this earnest lad or objecting to his simple vernacular of the sea. He spoke as the Spirit gave him utterance. So did they all. One young man asked counsel in regard to the rightfulness of his discharging some prescribed duties in a government office on the Sabbath mornings. The leader answered his question briefly, and a brother offered prayer that God would guide aright his perplexed child, would enable him to "do right even if it cost him his daily bread," and would deliver the land from Sabbath desecration in high places.

When his prayer was ended, a tremulous, stammering voice was heard in the further room for a moment, and then it stopped. There was a breathless pause. Everyone felt for the young beginner. Everyone wanted to help him out. He began again, hesitated, stammered out a few words brokenly; at last he said, "O Lord, Thou knowest I cannot tell what I want to say; but Thou hearest even what I do not say. Have mercy on my poor soul, for Christ's sake. Amen." An audible sob broke out throughout the whole apartment. Then outspoke a gray-headed veteran, in tones like old Andrew Peden's among the Covenanters of the Highlands. The old man went into his prayer like Gideon into the battle with Midian (Judg 7). The sword of faith gleamed in his right hand; the light shot forth as from the shivered pitchers, and the whole host of doubts, and sins, and fears were scattered like chaff at the breath of the gale. How he took us all on eagles' wings heavenward! How he enthroned the glorified Lamb! And the close of his rapturous outbreak was in a "sevenfold chorus of hallelujahs, and harping symphonies."

A Model Prayer Meeting

When the old man's prayer was ended (it was the *seventh* prayer offered during that one busy, blessed hour), the time had arrived for closing the service. The leader touched his bell and read the doxology. We were all in the very frame for that most celestial of strains—glorious *Old Hundred*[3]—that magnificent battle-hymn to which Luther marched against principalities and powers, and spiritual wickedness in high places. Immortal is that strain, like him who gave it birth. There is not a Christian's tomb in all our land where repose not the silent lips that once sang that matchless tune. If any of earth's music shall be heard amid the "new songs" of Paradise, be assured that the one surviving piece that shall outlive the judgment will be that "king of sacred airs," Old Hundred. With this ancient song upon our lips, we closed our service, spent a few moments in hand shakings, in introducing strangers, in cordial heart-greetings; and so ended a model prayer meeting.

The spirit that pervaded the meeting was too intensely earnest for phraseology as sapless and dry as last year's corn husks, and at the same time too reverential for affectations and flippancy. We lingered about the hallowed spot, loth to go away. But for the rigid rule that restricted the service to a single hour, we might have tarried until midnight, praying and singing praises to God. And as we turned reluctantly homeward, more than one gratefully said, "Truly the Lord was in this place" (Gen 28:16). Why may not every church of Christ have one or more just such model prayer meetings?

---

3. Old Hundred, or Old Hundredth, is a familiar hymn tune that was commonly used to sing Psalm 100. It is also the tune sung to the words of "Praise God from Whom All Blessings Flow."

Chapter 9

Revivals

BY THE WORD "REVIVAL" we commonly describe such a condition of a church that Christians are more than ordinarily active and spiritually minded, and as a result, the conversions of the impenitent are more than ordinarily numerous. Whatever the other characteristics may be, two phenomena are essential to a genuine revival—the Holy Spirit quickens believers and the Holy Spirit regenerates sinners. The power of the work of grace may be estimated by the degree with which the Divine Spirit produces these blessed results. Never forget, my young brother, that the foremost factor, the indispensable agent is that same Spirit which was poured out with such marvelous results on the day of Pentecost.

After a long pastoral experience and frequent labors in revivals I confess that there is much that is utterly mysterious in regard to them. Our God is a sovereign. He often seems to withhold His converting power at the very time when according to our calculations, we ought to expect it. I have had many disappointments of this kind. On the other hand, several copious showers of heavenly blessings have descended when we were not expecting them. The first revival that ever visited my ministry (in my little church at Burlington, New Jersey) began at a time of deep discouragement;

it began too in a single act of one godly woman. The most remarkable work of grace that I have ever enjoyed was in the Lafayette Avenue Church, Brooklyn (in 1866); and that commenced during the "week of prayer." There were no extraordinary efforts made, no peculiar expectations of a revival were discernible, no outside help was called for, from the beginning to the end. In both cases the showers burst upon us suddenly.

It has not been my custom to send for Evangelists to do the work which the Master has committed to me. Eighteen years ago, I invited my beloved friend, Mr. Dwight L. Moody, to come and conduct a series of special services in one of our Mission chapels. He prepared there the first "Bible Readings" which he ever delivered; and after a few days of patient effort, a fire was kindled which spread through the parent congregation, and over one hundred souls were hopefully converted. In 1887 my church united with several neighboring churches in inviting that very earnest and discreet evangelist, the Rev. B. Fay Mills,[1] to conduct public meetings during about three weeks, and his faithful preaching produced some happy results. There is often a prodigious temptation to pastors and churches to shirk their own responsibility, and to send off after somebody to come and do their work for them. The minister thinks that "perhaps a new voice may wake up the sleepers," or his officers may suggest that some "novelty will draw the people out" and accordingly an invitation is sent to Mr. A—, the evangelist, or Mr. B—, the Bible reader, or the Rev. Mr. C—, the "revivalist," to come and inaugurate some special services. Far be it from me to speak disparagingly of some faithful, godly minded itinerants who go about preaching the pure gospel, or holding "Bible readings," or conducting various meetings for arousing sinners or edifying believers. I sometimes wish that they would carry their torches oftener into the darkness of neglected regions and not spend so much time in setting their extra lamps in pulpits and prayer rooms that are already well lighted. One of the dangers of importing outside laborers is that it tends to belittle and disparage the installed shepherds of the flock. An idea is becoming quite current that the

1. Benjamin Fay Mills (1857–1916), popular traveling evangelist of the day.

pastor may plod on in his routine of expounding God's Word, visiting his flock, comforting the sick and sorrowing, and burying the dead; but if souls are to be converted, then somebody must be sent for whose profession it is to convert people. He is sent for as a farmer whose wheat is ripe goes after the owner of a patent "Reaper" to bring his machine that will cut and bind the grain with the utmost dispatch. Surely, if nobody else can bring a new gospel or a new Redeemer, or another Holy Spirit than the One that is promised to the prayer of faith, why should a faithful and zealous pastor look anywhere else than heavenward? Sometimes it may be wise to employ itinerant heralds of the gospel; but commonly a minister had better sow his own seed and reap his own harvests.

We must bear in mind that God always means to be God. He bestows spiritual blessings when He pleases, how He pleases, and where He pleases. We may labor, we may pray, we may "plant," but we must not dictate. Sometimes a godly pastor—greatly troubled by the low state of religion in his church—sets in motion some special machinery to produce a revival. It comes to nothing. The wheels whirl for awhile, but there is "no living Spirit within the wheels" (Ezek 1:20–21). Never, in my whole life, have I arranged any peculiar measures to produce a revival, which have been successful. The shower of blessings has descended upon us when I have been preaching God's Word in my usual way and when the church has been in what may be called an "average condition." Whatever the experience of other pastors has been, this has been my experience.

∾

(1) In the first place, then, I would advise you, my brother, not to talk too much about a "revival." You will wear out the very word. Lay hold of your heaven appointed work of preaching the whole gospel and soak it in prayer; keep at it and do your utmost to keep your people at work; and then commit the results to God. Do not worry; do not become disheartened; do not scold your people; do not undertake anything but the fearless, faithful, and loving discharge of duty to your Master and to dying souls. Constantly

present the great vital truths of the inspired Book—such as human depravity, the remedy for sin, the atonement of Jesus Christ, justification by faith, the character and claims of Jesus, the Bible rules of clean living, the final judgment, and future retributions. Waste no time in defending your Bible; *preach it* and let it defend itself! Preach sound doctrine fervently, and with lively, helpful illustrations. A revival that is not founded on Bible truth is a blaze of pine shavings and will end in smoke. You should mingle your instructive discourses with frequent arguments and tender appeals to the unconverted. Say as little as you can about "revivals"—and keep your own eyes and those of your people upon "no man but Jesus only!" (Matt 17:8). Deal with sin fearlessly; press home upon the consciences of your hearers the tremendous claims of God, the necessity of immediate repentance and acceptance of the Savior. Keep your people at personal work for the welfare of others and for the salvation of souls.

∽

(2) Watch, with open eye and ear, for the first tokens of a special manifestation of the Spirit's presence; be on the lookout, and the moment that you detect such a manifestation, follow it up promptly. One afternoon, when I was out making calls, I discovered that in two or three families there were anxious seekers after salvation. I immediately called together the officers of my church, stated to them my discoveries, and we instituted a series of meetings for almost every evening, and followed them with conversations with inquirers. A large ingathering of souls rewarded our efforts and prayers. Without any noise, or violent excitement, or "sensational" devices, the good work went steadily on for months, and there was no reaction after it. People did not flock together to hear a noted preacher; they came to hear *preaching* of the Word (which is a mightily different thing). All the time, too, there was abundant and fervent prayer by God's people. When revivals die down, they die from the want of humble, persistent supplication, and the lack of persistent laboring and living for the Lord. The church gets satisfied with the harvest, and the harvesting stops. When we cease

to cooperate with the Holy Spirit, then the grieved and neglected Spirit withholds His converting power.

∾

(3) While it is true that we finite creatures cannot predict the times or seasons of the Spirit's special presence, yet it is always right to be praying for an outpouring of the power from on high. The late Dr. Thos. H. Skinner[2] (a remarkably humble and holy man) told me that two or three of his elders, in Philadelphia, met in his study to prostrate themselves before God and to ask for a baptism of the Spirit. They emptied themselves and prayed to be filled with Christ. He did fill them. Then they interceded most fervently for the awakening and conversion of sinners. Presently a most powerful revival shook the whole church like the mighty blast which filled the upper room at Pentecost. Mr. Finney[3] tells us that for fourteen successive winters there was a rich spiritual blessing brought down upon a certain church just because it was the custom of the church officers to "pray fervently for their minister far into the night before each Sabbath." Those wise, godly men honored Christ's ambassador, honored His gospel, honored their own duty, and felt their own responsibility. They did not run off to Egypt for help. The prayer-hearing God honored *them*.

∾

(4) When the influences of the Spirit are recognized in your congregation in any unwonted[4] degree, you must be on the alert and be prompt and untiring in your cooperation with the Divine Agent. The secret of success in a revival is to cooperate with the Holy Spirit. Therefore, you will be praying most fervently for His guidance. Appoint as many services of prayer as can be profitably attended. During the remarkable revival in my church (in 1866),

2. Thomas H. Skinner (1791–1871), Presbyterian pastor and founder of Union Theological Seminary.

3. Charles G. Finney (1792–1875), the leading preacher of the Second Great Awakening.

4. Unaccustomed or unusual.

the following program of services was carried out. It may give you some hints if I reproduce it here.

On Monday evenings our young people held their regular weekly gathering, which was very crowded, and was followed by a service for inquirers. On Tuesday evening, Thursday evening, and Friday evening, there was a general prayer service, followed by inquiry meetings. On Wednesday evening I usually preached as clearly and pungently as I possibly could—sometimes to backsliders, sometimes to the impenitent, and sometimes to awakened sinners who were seeking salvation. This service, like all the others, was followed by a cordial invitation to all inquirers to go into a large adjoining room for personal conversation and prayer. I found a vast benefit from this plan. It revealed to me just *who* were awakened, and the very act of going into that room *as inquirers* had a certain strengthening and compacting influence upon those who were awakened. It was a step, and a step in the right direction. If pride and self-conceit were somewhat humbled by this step, all the better. In addition to these evening services there was an afternoon meeting of young lads (for an hour) and another afternoon meeting of young ladies. Both these services were in charge of experienced Christians, and were devoted to prayer, praise, and free conversation.

∾

(5) The inquiry meetings during a season of revival are so vitally and critically important, that no rash, inexperienced, or fanatical person ought to be admitted to converse with inquirers. By the fanatical I mean all such people as are (in Scotch phrase) "clean daft"[5] with some spiritual hobby of their own. I always conducted the inquiry meetings myself and called to my aid certain men and women who possessed both grace and good sense. (The two are not *always* found in combination.) In the solemn work of the inquiry room no small artifices were allowed. I aimed to discover just what hindrance was in the path of each inquirer. It is a great

---

5. Silly or foolish.

point for a sinner to discover what it is that keeps him from surrendering to Christ. If it be some habit or some evil practice, then he must give it up. If some heart sin, then he must yield—even if it be like plucking out a right eye or lopping off a right hand. Commonly the chief hindrance lies in a wicked, stubborn heart. It was my aim, and ever has been, to convince the awakened person that, unless he or she was willing to give that heart to Jesus, and to "do the will" of Jesus, there was no hope for them. We must shut the soul up to Christ!

Of course, the Word of God is as indispensable in an inquiry meeting as a compass on board of a ship. It is well to have certain passages so familiar to the mind that you can turn to them instantly and read them to the one who is seeking for light. The healing of blind Bartimaeus (Mark 10:46–52) and the conversation of Christ with Nicodemus (John 3:1–21) I have always found helpful in guiding inquirers. When you use the inspired directions of God's Word you are sure that you are right, and you may always confidently ask for a blessing on God's own instrument. You ought to converse with each person individually. If time forbids as full discussion as the case demands, then appoint some hour for further conversation at the person's house or your own study. During a season of awakening, you must not allow anything to call you away from your parish—especially any "lecturing" or money-making expedition—and you will probably find it necessary to devote half of every day to thorough visitations and conversations from house to house. Do not begrudge the time required to guide a perplexed or halting soul into the kingdom. Hand-picked apples keep the longest. Individual labor with each individual soul is indispensable. The book of the "Acts" of the apostles is such a record. Those early Christians understood their personal responsibility and the power of personal effort. Peter goes right after Cornelius (Acts 10:1–33); Philip talks directly to Queen Candace's royal treasurer (Acts 8:26–40); Paul answers the Philippian jailor's questions face to face (Acts 16:25–34), and Aquila and Priscilla have a great Bible class in the person of the eloquent Apollos (Acts 18:24–28). If the Son of God would devote so much time to the Jewish ruler who came to him by night (John 3:1–15), and to a poor soul-smirched woman at the well of Sychar (John 4:1–42), surely we ought to spare no time or toil in leading an immortal soul out of darkness into the daylight.

∾

(6) "Had I better ask those who are seeking Christ to rise in a public meeting?" To this question I would reply that the method of inviting anxious inquirers to rise for special prayer has been adopted by many very wise pastors; it has been blessed with many glorious results. During the first half of my ministry, I requested inquirers to remain after the service for conversation, or to go into a room by themselves. During later years I have often requested those who wished to be prayed for to manifest that desire by rising. So many happy results have followed this measure that, on the whole, I approve of it. But great discretion must be used, or else a very solemn step will be perverted into a flippant and careless formality. Be very careful to set before your auditors just what is involved in "rising for prayer," and make your invitation not only affectionate but so clear that even the weakest may understand it. Let the prayer that is offered be direct, simple, and importunate. When the service is over those who have taken the public step of rising up should be conversed with in private. After an inquirer has made a firm decision for Christ, I have always encouraged them to make it known to others. A few touching words from a newborn soul will often thrill a meeting like the sight of a Lazarus lifted from the tomb. It quickens the faith of God's people wonderfully to hear the "new song" from a soul that has been dead in trespasses and sin. Unless young converts begin to testify for Christ at once, they are apt to be tongue-tied all their lives.

∾

(7) The preaching during a revival should be steeped in Holy Scripture and saturated with prayer. You cannot be too simple, too earnest, too close in your applications, or too clear in your

illustrations. President Finney—a king of revival preachers—used to subsoil his auditors' hearts by a prodigiously powerful presentation of every sinner's personal guilt before God. He put his plough in deep—"up to the beam"—and it made ripping work in the conscience. His chief aim was to make every unconverted hearer realize that he was a sinner against infinite holiness and love; that sin was exceedingly damnable; that it should be repented of and abandoned straightway; and that the sinner should turn immediately to God who would grant abundant pardon through Jesus Christ, the all-sufficient Savior of every man who trusts in Him. Pungent convictions followed such preaching; the conversions were usually as clean-cut as the stamp of the die on a gold eagle from the mint. We need more of such thorough work in the pulpits of these days. The keynote of John the Baptist's preaching, of Jesus Christ's first preaching, and of apostolic preaching was "repent—*repent!*" (Matt 3:2; 4:17; Acts 2:38; 17:30–31). You must bear in mind that "repentance unto life is a saving grace whereby a sinner, out of a true sense of his sin and apprehension of the mercy of God in Christ, doth with grief and hatred of his sin, *turn from it unto God* with full purpose of and endeavor after new obedience."[6] Can any step be more vital, or any duty be more peremptory than this? Do not be afraid of preaching with too much of the plainness of love; do not hesitate to make every soul that is in the wrong place feel uncomfortable. The more deeply a man feels his guilt, his weakness, and his desert of punishment, the sooner will he flee to the crucified Lamb of God. That revival will leave the most enduring results which sends every awakened soul to "Jesus only" (Matt 17:8)—and which draws the church into the closest daily imitation of its holy and loving Lord.

6. From the *Westminster Shorter Catechism*, Question 87.

Chapter 10

Drawing the Bow at a Venture

AMONG THE MANY DELIGHTFUL prayer meetings held during a revival in the town of B—, there was one which I never can forget, and which some souls, I trust, will remember in that hour when the redeemed shall be summoned in to the marriage supper of the Lamb. It was held in a private dwelling, and the rooms were thronged. The house was as silent as the grave when I entered, and many were sitting with their heads bowed and their faces covered. An awful solemnity hung over the little assembly, for the Spirit of the Lord "was in that place." An hour was spent in singing two or three inviting hymns, and while two aged men (both far up the Delectable Mountains[1]), poured forth fervent prayers, which were interrupted by frequent sobs and exclamations. When the benediction was pronounced, a request was made that all who desired private conversation on the state of their souls would remain. The whole assembly settled back again, as one man, into their seats! The scene was overwhelming. Some of those before me were professed Christians, some had been openly profane, many of them

---

1. A reference from Bunyan, *The Pilgrim's Progress.*

were strangers. It was evident that a word must be spoken to all, and the bow be "drawn at a venture."[2]

Near me sat a young female dressed in black, whose face betokened a deep solemnity. I had never seen her before and supposed her to be a member of a neighboring church, who had come in to unite her prayers with our own. Approaching her respectfully, I ventured to ask her if "she had any hope that she was a child of God?" Her head dropped in a moment; she burst into tears, and in her deep emotion her answer to me was not intelligible. With a kind word of exhortation I left her, and after a little inquiry I learned that she had been for a long time utterly thoughtless, and a perpetual neglecter of the house of God. At our next meeting I saw the same face again, but sadder than before. At the end of a fortnight (one of indescribable anguish to her struggling soul), the cloud left her brow, and the serenity of a peace that passeth understanding sat like a dove upon her happy countenance. She is now a humble and consistent member of the fold of Christ.

Farther on was a timid and retiring young member of my congregation, with whom I had never had an opportunity for conversation. As she sat with her face covered, I addressed a few pointed inquiries to her and turned away. The next day a member of my church called upon me to say that the person whom I had addressed as impenitent and thoughtless, was a church member before I came to B—, but her name had either been omitted from the record or confounded with that of two others in the congregation bearing the same name. I sent the necessary explanation to her and thought no more about it. When nearly a month had elapsed, the same person who had before waited on me, stopped me one evening at the church door and said, "I wish you would call on M— T— and endeavor to calm her. She is in a state of utter despair. Those remarks that you made to her in the inquiry

2. A reference to the story in 1 Kgs 22:34 where Ahab was killed when "a certain man drew a bow at a venture and smote the king of Israel," meaning he drew his bow and shot it randomly but it hit the mark intended by the Lord. The language of "drawing a bow at a venture" is used here to refer to speaking to people at random, which may end up being used of the Lord to accomplish his own intended purposes.

meeting by mistake have troubled her ever since. She fears now that she never was a true Christian, and after a long struggle with her pride, she can no longer conceal her anguish. I fear, sir, that she will lose her reason." I called at once, as requested, and found the unhappy young woman the picture of despair. It was a long time before her weeping eyes could be turned toward Calvary, or she could be persuaded that there was mercy left for one who had so long done despite to the Spirit of Divine grace. But the wound which the stray arrow—guided by infinite wisdom—had made, was at length healed. The Master's gentle voice whispered, "Peace." She went on her way rejoicing, and though her eye may never rest on this humble volume, she can hardly forget to her dying day that interview in the inquiry meeting.

During the progress of the revival, it was pleasant to hear from one how he had been awakened by a tract handed to him "at a venture"—how another had been aroused by some particular passage in a discourse—and how some had been reached by truths that were aimed at others than themselves. "Dr. C— preached entirely *at me* last evening," said a young man to me one Monday morning. "He reached my own case exactly, and I never heard such a sermon before." It is certain that he never heard before with such a spirit as then; and for that discourse he will doubtless bless Redeeming Love when the ransomed host shall shout their Harvest Home!

Fainting and desponding minister of Christ! Who shall dare to tell you, when you have come back from preaching the cross boldly and earnestly, that many an arrow may not have pierced the waiting souls around you? You may not have seen its flight. You may have heard no outcry of the wounded soul. You may have seen no tears and heard no groans. You may never hear of them in this world. But in the great day of retribution, you shall stand as God's appointed archer, with the trophies of redeeming grace about you—and stars shall blaze in the coronet of your rejoicing, which are now unseen save by Him who seeth in secret and rewardeth openly.

Chapter 11

Where To Be a Pastor

"SHOULD A YOUNG MINISTER take a large church or a small one for his first pastorate?" Some cynical persons might respond to this question that a man fresh from the theological seminary, who has had no experience, had better "take" whatever he can get. For it is true that some men who have risen to great eminence have not found it easy to secure a very favorable hearing at the start. Another person might respond that a young man whose ambition led him to "seek great things for himself" (Jer 45:5) would very likely be forced to content himself with small things. Certainly, the surest way for any man to secure a wide field is for him to fill full and overflow a narrow field. All that any licentiate of real force and consecrated heart should reasonably ask is to find some pulpit, high or humble, in which to begin his heaven-directed work. When God calls a man to the gospel ministry, he is very apt to get calls from his fellow men to preach that gospel. The demand exceeds the supply.

Supposing that a young man of abilities and fervent piety were permitted to choose between two calls, the one to a large church and the other to a small one, which of the two should he prefer for his first pastorate? I answer unhesitatingly, the small church.

In Scotland the rule has been to locate the "apprentices" in a rural parish and then let them work their way up into the large towns. A wise custom it is too. Thus the great Chalmers began in the little parish of Kilmany; Dr. Norman McLeod's[1] first settlement was among the farmers and weavers of Loudon; the eloquent Guthrie[2] had hard work to get the humble parish of Arbirot; and the sainted McCheyne commenced his wonderful ministry at Dundee as the pastor of a new colony of artisans and day laborers. There are several strong reasons why a small church is to be preferred at the outset. And I shall always thank God that my own lot was cast during my early ministry in a little parish of about one hundred souls, a considerable portion of whom were shoemakers, gardeners, and coachmen. A distinguished lawyer who attended my church during the summer months used to say to me, "I want you to preach the gospel so simply and plainly that my coachman and gardener can understand you as well as I do." That sensible advice did me, as our Southern friends say, "a heap of good."

∾

(1) The first argument for a small parish is that it gives a young minister a better opportunity to study individuals. He has fewer persons to count, and he counts every man and every woman; yes, and if he is wise, every child. The most profitable study for every minister, next to his Bible, is human character. The misfortune with many of our young ministers in these days is that they know more about books than about human nature. When there are but few individuals in his flock, the pastor gets a deeper insight into each one; and he also learns more thoroughly that mighty lesson, the infinite value of one immortal soul. A crowd is an inspiring object for me to preach to; an individual soul brought into close and living contact is an inspiring personage to preach to me. In a big city we deal with the masses; in a quiet rural or village parish a

---

1. Norman McLeod (1812–1872), prominent Scottish pastor. Loudon, where he served, is in Ayrshire, Scotland.

2. Thomas Guthrie (1803–1873), leading Scottish preacher of his day. The village which Cuyler refers to as "Arbirot" is most often called "Arbirlot."

pastor deals with each man, woman, or child. That minister rarely gains a great hold or exerts a great power over a congregation, who has no personal hold on the various persons who compose that congregation.

∾

(2) A second argument for a small parish is that it gives the young beginner more time for uninterrupted study and more time to think. Almost no great immortal work has been produced amid the pressure of a large pastorate. Jonathan Edwards could not have written the *Freedom of the Will*, John Bunyan could not have written *The Pilgrim's Progress*, and Charles Hodge could not have prepared his massive *Systematic Theology*, if they had been the pastors of big city churches, with their doorbells playing a perpetual St. Vitus dance.[3] Many a city pastor has maintained himself mainly on the good stock laid in during his early settlement in some quiet neighborhood. A young minister must learn the use of his tools. He must learn how to think and how to put his thoughts into the most effective shape. If he ever expects to be a vigorous, meaty, instructive, and enduring extempore preacher, he must first spend several years in carefully writing out his discourses. A small church will afford him the best opportunity to lay good, broad, solid foundations by deep meditation, deep study of the Word, and of fertilizing books and deep study of human nature. Nearly all the greatest American ministers have commenced their careers in small or in secluded parishes. Dr. Archibald Alexander once said to us in his Princeton lecture room, "Young gentlemen, do not be ambitious to begin in the city; I never knew but one man who did this and held out through a long life without breaking down."

The strain upon pastors grows heavier every year. The multiplication of societies, enterprises, and "causes," (some of them without much effect); the tendency to overload churches with what does not belong to them, the encroachments and the competitions of the busy world about us, make the life of an earnest, spiritual

---

3. St. Vitus dance, now called Sydenham chorea, is a disease characterized by rapid, involuntary, and irregular movements of the muscles.

pastor no holiday business. Young brethren, if you know when you are well off, do not itch for a call to a large town; and do not lose one golden hour that you may now be spending in some modest little corner of the Master's vast vineyard. If you have bread to put into your mouths, and nutritious books to study, and immortal souls to win for Christ, be thankful and buckle to your work. Time enough to shoulder up the bullock when you have learned to carry the calf. Bend your whole undivided strength upon your first charge, even if it does not contain over one hundred precious souls; and remember that a single soul for whom Jesus died is a tremendous trust. Those who are overloaded too early in life break down the soonest. Therefore, if both a large church and a small one was offered at the same time to any young minister, it would be the highest proof of his sagacity for him to accept the latter. He would be far more likely to hold a position of commanding influence and usefulness fifteen or twenty years afterward.

∾

There are many other practical questions that I should like to discuss—such as the relations of a pastor to the Sunday School, the methods of receiving members into the church, and of dealing with those who may require ecclesiastical discipline, the performance of marriage rites, and the administration of the sacraments. But the limits which I had prescribed for myself forbid my consideration of these and several other kindred topics. My chief aim has been to set forth the great principles and purposes which should animate and inspire the sacred office of a Christian pastor. How far I have been enabled (with the Divine assistance) to realize my own ideal of pastoral labor, will appear in the following discourse—which I would modestly present as the closing chapter of this little volume.

Chapter 12

The Joys of the Christian Ministry

A Valedictory Discourse delivered to the
Lafayette Avenue Church, April 6th, 1890.[1]

I INVITE YOUR ATTENTION this morning to the nineteenth and twentieth verses of the second chapter of Paul's First Epistle to the Thessalonians:

> For what is our hope, or joy, or crown of rejoicing? Are not even ye in the presence of our Lord Jesus Christ at His coming? For ye are our glory and joy.

These words were written by the most remarkable man in the annals of the Christian church. Great interest is attached to them from the fact that they are part of the first inspired epistle that Paul ever wrote. Nay, more. The letter to the church of Thessalonica is probably the earliest as to date of all the books of the New Testament. Paul was then at Corinth, about fifty-two years old, in the full vigor of his splendid prime. His spiritual son, Timothy, brings him tidings from the infant church in Thessalonica that awakens

---

1. The majority of this farewell discourse has been left intact, but there are brief portions that have been removed due to the fact that they were of such a specific historical and/or personal nature that they would have very little meaning or value for the modern reader.

his solicitude. He yearns to go and see them, but he cannot; so he determines to write to them; and one day he lays aside his tent needle, seizes his pen, and, when that pen touches the papyrus sheet, the New Testament begins. The apostle's great, warm heart kindles and blazes as he goes on, and at length bursts out in this impassioned utterance: "Ye are my glory and joy!" (verse 20).

Paul, I thank thee for a thousand things, but for nothing do I thank thee more than for that golden sentence. In these thrilling words, the greatest of Christian pastors, rising above the poverty, homelessness, and scorn that surrounded him, reaches forth his hand and grasps his royal diadem. No man shall rob the aged hero of his crown. No chaplet worn by a Roman conqueror in the hour of his brightest triumph, rivals the coronal that Pastor Paul sees flashing before his eyes. It is a crown blazing with stars; every star an immortal soul plucked from the darkness of sin into the light and liberty of a child of God. Poor, is he? He is making many rich. Despised, is he? He wouldn't change places with Caesar. Homeless, is he? His citizenship is in heaven, where he will find myriads whom he can meet and say to them: "Ye, ye are my glory and joy" (verse 20). Sixteen centuries after Paul uttered these words, John Bunyan reechoed them when he said:

> I have counted as if I had goodly buildings in the places where my spiritual children were born. My heart has been so wrapt up in this excellent work that I accounted myself more honored of God than if He had made me emperor of all the world, or the lord of all the glory of the earth without it. He that converteth a sinner from the error of his ways doth save a soul from death; and they that be wise shall shine as the brightness of the firmament.[2]

Now, the great apostle expressed what every ambassador of Christ constantly experiences when in the thick of the Master's work. His are the joys of acquisition. His purse may be scanty, his teaching may be humble, and the field of his labor may be so obscure that no bulletins of his achievements are ever proclaimed to an admiring world. Difficulties may sadden and discouragement

---

2. From John Bunyan, *Grace Abounding to the Chief of Sinners*.

bring him to his knees; but I tell you that obscure, toiling man of God has a joy vouchsafed to him that a Frederick[3] or a Marlborough[4] never knew on the field of bloody triumph, or that a Rothschild[5] never dreams of in his mansions of splendor, nor an Astor[6] with his stores of gold. Every nugget of fresh truth discovered makes him happier than one who has found golden spoil. Every attentive auditor is a delight; every look of interest on a human countenance flashes back to illuminate his own. Above all, when the tears of penitence course down a cheek and a returning soul is led by him to the Savior, there is great joy in heaven over a repentant wanderer, and a joy in that minister's heart too exquisite to utter. Then he is repaid in full measure, pressed down, running over into his bosom.

Converted souls are jewels in the caskets of faithful parents, teachers, and pastors. They shall flash in the diadem which the Righteous Judge shall give them in that great day. Ah! it is when an ambassador of Christ sees an army of young converts and listens to the first utterances of their newborn love, and when he presides at a communion table and sees his spiritual offspring gathered around him, more true joy that faithful pastor feels than "Caesar with a Senate at his heels."[7] Rutherford,[8] of Scotland, only voiced the yearnings of every true pastor's heart when he exclaimed: "Oh, how rich were I if I could obtain of my Lord the salvation of you all! What a prey had I gotten to have you all caught in Christ's net.

---

3. Frederick the Great (1712–1786), King of Prussia, known for his military triumphs in the Silesian wars.

4. The Duke of Marlborough (1650–1722), British military general known for his success in the War of the Spanish Succession.

5. The Rothschilds were a wealthy family originally from Frankfurt and the most famous of all European banking dynasties. During the nineteenth century, the Rothschild family possessed the largest private fortune in the world.

6. John Jacob Astor (1763–1848), German-born businessman and investor who came to America and made his fortune in the fur trade.

7. From William Shakespeare, *Julius Caesar*.

8. Samuel Rutherford (1600–1661), Scottish pastor of Anwoth and professor of divinity at St. Andrews.

My witness is above, that your heaven would be the two heavens to me, and the salvation of you all would be two salvations to me."[9]

Yet, my beloved people, when I recall the joy of my forty-four years of public ministry, I often shudder at the fact of how near I came to losing it. For very many months my mind was balancing between the pulpit and the attractions of a legal and political career. A single hour in a village prayer meeting turned the scale. But perhaps behind it all a beloved mother's prayers were moving the mysterious hand that touched the poised balance, and made souls outweigh silver and eternity outweigh time.

Would that I could lift up my voice this morning in every academy, college, and university on this broad continent. I would say to every gifted Christian youth, "God and humanity have need of you." He who redeemed you by His precious blood has a sovereign right to the best brains and the most persuasive tongues and the highest culture. Why crowd into the already overcrowded professions? The only occupation in America that is not overdone is the occupation of serving Jesus Christ and saving souls. I do not affirm that a Christian cannot serve his Master in any other sphere or calling than the gospel ministry; but I do affirm that the ambition for worldly gains and worldly honors is sluicing the very heart of God's church, and drawing out today much of the church's best blood in their greedy outlets. And I fearlessly declare that when the most splendid talent has reached the loftiest round on the ladder of promotion, that round is many rungs lower than a pulpit in which a consecrated tongue proclaims a living Christianity to a dying world. What Lord Eldon[10] from the bar, what Webster[11] from the Senate chamber, what Sir Walter Scott[12] from

9. From Samuel Rutherford, "Letter to the Parishioners at Anwoth (July 1637)," *The Letters of Samuel Rutherford.*

10. Lord Eldon (1751–1838), British lawyer and politician considered by many to be the greatest lawyer of his time.

11. Daniel Webster (1782–1852), American politician considered to be one of the nation's great orators.

12. Sir Walter Scott (1771–1832), Scottish novelist, poet, and playwright.

the realms of romance, what Darwin[13] from the field of science, what monarch from Wall Street or Lombard Street can carry his laurels or his gold up to the judgment seat and say, "These are my joy and crown"? The laurels and the gold will be dust—ashes. But if so humble a servant of Jesus Christ as your pastor can ever point to the gathered flock arrayed in white before the celestial throne, then he may say, "What is my hope, or joy, or crown of rejoicing? Are not even ye in the presence of Christ at His coming?" (verses 19–20).

Good friends, I have told you what aspirations led me to the pulpit as a place in which to serve my Master; and I thank Christ, the Lord, for putting me into the ministry. The forty-four years I have spent in that office have been unspeakably happy. Many a far better man has not been as happy from causes beyond control. He may have had to contend with feeble health as I never have; or a despondent temperament, as I never have; or have struggled to maintain a large household on a slender purse; he may have been placed in a stubborn field, where the gospel was shattered to pieces on flinty hearts. From all such trials a kind providence has delivered your pastor.

My ministry began in a very small church. For that I am thankful. Let no young minister covet a large parish at the outset. The clock that is not content to strike one will never strike twelve. In that little parish at Burlington, New Jersey, I had opportunity for the two most valuable studies for any minister—God's Book and individual hearts. My next call was to organize and serve an infant church in Trenton, New Jersey, and for that I am thankful. Laying the foundation of a new church affords capital tuition in spiritual masonry, and the walls of that church have stood firm and solid for forty years. The crowning mercy of my Trenton ministry was this, that one Sunday while I was watering the flock, a goodlier vision than that of Rebecca appeared at the well's mouth, and the sweet sunshine of that presence has never departed from the pathway of my life. To this hour the prosaic old capital of New Jersey has a

13. Charles Darwin (1809–1882), British scientist famous for his theory of evolution.

halo of poetry floating over it, and I never go through it without waving a benediction from the passing train.

The next stage of my life's work was a seven year's pastorate of Market Street Church in the City of New York. To those seven years of hard and happy labor I look back with joy. The congregation swarmed with young men, many of whom have risen to prominence in the commercial and religious life of the great metropolis. The name of Market Street is graven indelibly on my heart. I rejoice that the quaint old edifice still stands and welcomes every Sabbath a congregation of landsmen and of sailors. During the year 1858 occurred the great revival, when a mighty wind from heaven filled every house where the people of God were sitting, and the glorious work of that revival kept many of us busy for six months, night and day.

Early in the year 1860 a signal was made to me from this side of the East River. It came from a brave little band then known as the Park Presbyterian Church, who had never had any installed pastor. The signal at first was unheeded; but a higher than human hand seemed to be behind it, and I had only to obey. That little flock stood like the man of Macedonia, saying, "Come over and help us" (Acts 16:9), and after I had seen the vision immediately I decided to come, assuredly concluding that God had called me to preach the gospel unto them.

This morning my memory goes back to that chilly, stormy April Sunday when my labors began as your first pastor. About two hundred and fifty people, full of grace and grit, gathered on that Easter morning to see how God could roll away stones that for two years had blocked their path with discouragement. My first message many of you remember. It was, "I determined not to know anything among you save Jesus Christ and Him crucified" (1 Cor 2:2). Of that little company the large majority has departed. Many of them are among the white-robed that now behold their risen Lord in glory. Of the seventeen church officers—elders, deacons, and trustees—then in office, who greeted me that day, only four are living, and of that number only one, Mr. Albion P. Higgins, is now a member of this congregation. I wonder how many there are here this morning that gathered before my pulpit on that Easter Sunday thirty years ago? As many of you as there are present that were at that service thirty years ago will do me a favor if you will rise in your pews.

(Thirteen people here stood up). God bless you! If it hadn't been for you, this ark would never have been built.

Ah! we had happy days in that modest chapel. The tempest of civil war was raging,[14] with Lincoln's steady hand at the helm. We got our share of the gale; but we set our storm-sails, and every one that could handle ropes stood at his or her place. Just think of the money contributions that small church made during the first year of my pastorate—$20,000, not in paper, but in gold. The little band in that chapel was not only generous in donations but valiant in spirit, and it was under the gracious shower of a revival that we removed into this edifice on the 16th March, 1862 . . .

. . . There is one department of ministerial labor that has had a peculiar attraction to me and afforded me peculiar joy. Pastoral work has always been my passion. It has been my rule to know everybody in this congregation, if possible, and seldom have I allowed a day to pass without a visit to some of your homes. I fancied that you cared more to have a warm-hearted pastor than a cold-blooded preacher, however intellectual. To carry out thoroughly a system of personal oversight, to visit every family, to stand by the sick and dying beds, to put one's self into sympathy with aching hearts and bereaved households, is a process that has swallowed up time, and I tell you it has strained the nerves prodigiously. Costly as the process has been, it has paid. If I have given sermons to you, I have got sermons from you. The closest tie that binds us together is that sacred tie that has been wound around the cribs in your nurseries, the couches in your sick chambers, the chairs at your fireside, and even the coffins that have borne away your precious dead. My fondest hope is that however much you may honor and love my successor in this pulpit, you will evermore keep a warm place in the chimney-corner of your hearts for the man that gave the best thirty years of his life to your service.

14. The American Civil War (1861–1865).

. . . House to house visitation has only been one hemisphere of the pastor's work. I have accordingly endeavored to guard the door of yonder study so that I might give undivided energy to preparation for this pulpit.

You know, my dear people, how I have preached and what I have preached. In spite of many interruptions, I have honestly handled each topic as best I could. The minister that foolishly runs races with himself is doomed to an early suicide. All that I claim for my sermons is that they have been true to God's Book and the cross of Jesus Christ, have been simple enough for a child to understand, and have been preached in full view of the judgment seat. I have aimed to keep this pulpit abreast of all great moral reforms and human progress, and the majestic marchings of the kingdom of King Jesus. The preparation of my sermons has been an unspeakable delight. The manna fell fresh every morning, and it had to me the sweetness of angels' food. Ah, there are many sharp pangs before me. None will be sharper than the hour that bids farewell to yonder blessed and beloved study. For twenty-eight years it has been my daily home—one of the dearest spots this side of heaven. From its walls have looked down upon me the inspiring faces of Chalmers, Charles Wesley, Spurgeon, Lincoln and Gladstone, Adams, Storrs, Guthrie, Newman Hall, and my beloved teachers, Charles Hodge and the Alexanders of Princeton. Thither your infant children have been brought on Sabbath mornings, awaiting their baptism. Thither your older children have come by hundreds to converse with me about the welfare of their souls. Thither have come all the candidates for admission to the fellowship of this church and have made there their confession of faith and their allegiance to Christ. Oh, what blessed interviews with inquirers have been held there! What sweet and happy fellowship with my successive bands of helpers, some of whom have joined the general assembly of the redeemed in glory. That hallowed study has been to me sometimes a Bochim of tears (Judg 2:1–5), and sometimes a Hermon,[15] when the vision was of no man save Jesus only (Matt 17:1–8). And the

15. Some people believe Mount Hermon was the site of Jesus' transfiguration (Matt 17:1–8), which is what Cuyler references above.

work there has been a wider one for a far wider multitude than these walls contain this morning. I have written there nearly all the hundreds of articles which have gone out through the religious press, over this country, over Great Britain, over Europe, over Australia, Canada, India, and New Zealand. During my ministry I have published about thirty-two hundred of these articles. Many of them have been gathered into books, many of them translated into Swedish, Spanish, Dutch, and other foreign tongues. They have made the scratch of a very humble pen audible to Christendom. The consecrated pen may be more powerful than the consecrated tongue. I devoutly thank God for having condescended to use my humble pen to the spread of His gospel; and I purpose with His help to spend much of the brief remainder of my life in preaching His glorious gospel through the press.

I am sincerely sorry that the necessities of this hour seem to require so personal a discourse this morning; but I must hide behind the example of the great apostle who gave me my text. Because he reviewed his ministry among his spiritual children of Thessalonica, I may be allowed to review my own too—standing here this morning under such peculiar circumstances. These thirty years have been to me years of unbounded joy. Sorrow I have had, when death paid four visits to my house; but the sorrow taught sympathy with the grief of others. Sins I have committed—too many of them; your patient love has never cast a stone. The faults of my ministry have been my own. The successes of my ministry have been largely due under God, to your cooperation; and, above all, to the amazing goodness of our heavenly Father. Looking my long pastorate squarely in the face, I think I can honestly say that I have been no man's man; I have never courted the rich, nor willfully neglected the poor; I have never blunted the sword of the Spirit lest it should cut your consciences, or concealed a truth that might save a soul. In no large church is there a perfect unanimity of tastes as to preaching. I do not doubt that there are some of you that are quite ready for the experiment of a new face in this pulpit, and perhaps there may be some who are lusting after the fat quail of elaborate or philosophic discourse. For thirty years I have tried to feed you on "nothing but manna" (Num 11:1–9). Whatever the difference of taste, you have always stood by me, true as steel. This has been your spiritual home; and you have loved your home, and you have drunk every Sunday from your own well; and though the water of life has not always been passed up to you in a richly embossed silver cup, it has drawn up the undiluted gospel from the inspired fountainhead. To hear the truth, to heed the truth, to "back" the truth with prayer and toil, has been the delight of the staunchest members of this church. Oh, the children of this church are inexpressibly dear to me! There are hundreds here today that never had any other home, nor ever knew any other pastor. I think I can say that "every baptism has baptized us into closer fellowship, every marriage has married us into closer union, every funeral that bore away your beloved dead, only bound us more strongly to the living." Every invitation from another church—and I have had some very attractive ones that I never told you about—every invitation from another church has always been promptly declined; for I long ago determined never to be pastor of any other than Lafayette Avenue Church.

What is my joy or crown of rejoicing? Are not even ye—ye—in the presence of Christ at His coming? Why, then, sunder a tie that is bound to every fiber of my inmost heart? I will answer you frankly. There must be no concealment or false pretexts between us. In the first place, as I told you two months ago, I had determined to make my thirtieth anniversary the terminal point of my present pastorate. I determined not to outstay my fullest capacity for the enormous work demanded here. The extent of that demanded work increases every twelve months. The requirements of preaching twice every Sunday, to visit the vast number of families directly connected with this church, attending funeral services, conferring with committees about Christian work of various kinds, and numberless other duties—all these requirements are prodigious. Thus far, by the Divine help, I have carried that load. My health today is as firm as usual; and I thank God that such forces of heart and brain as He has given me are unabated. The chronic catarrh[16]

16. Catarrh is a build-up of mucus in the nose, throat, and sinuses. Sufferers of chronic catarrh often feel as though they have a constant cold.

that long ago muffled my ears to many a strain of sweet music, has never made me too deaf to hear the sweet accents of your love. But I understand my constitution well enough to know that I could not carry the undivided load of this great church a great while longer without the risk of breaking down; and there must be no risk run with you or with myself. I also desire to assist you in transferring this magnificent vessel to the next pilot whom God shall appoint; and I wish to transfer it while it is well manned, well equipped, and on the clear sea of an unbroken financial and spiritual prosperity. No man shall ever say that I so far presumed on the generous kindness of this dear church as to linger here until I had outlived my usefulness.

For these reasons I present today my resignation of this sacred, precious charge. It is my honest desire and purpose that this day must terminate my present pastorate. For presenting this resignation I alone am responsible before God, before this church, and before the world. When you shall have accepted my resignation, the whole responsibility for the welfare of this beloved church will rest on your shoulders—not on mine. My earnest prayer is that you may soon be directed to the right man to be your minister, to one who shall unite all hearts and all hands, and carry forward the high and holy mission to which God has called you. He will find in me not a jealous critic, but a hearty ally in everything that he may regard for the welfare of this church.

As for myself, I do not propose to sit down on the veranda and watch the sun of life wheel downward in the west. The labors of a pen and of a ministry at large will afford me no lack of employment. The welfare of this church is inexpressibly dear to me—nothing is dearer to me this side of heaven. If, therefore, while this flock remains shepherdless, and in search of my successor, I can be of actual service to you in supplying at any time this pulpit or performing pastoral labor, that service, beloved, shall be performed cheerfully.

. . . For the first time in twenty-eight years this church is subjected to a severe strain. During all these years you had very smooth sailing. You have never been crippled by debt; you have never been distracted with quarrels, and you have never been without a pastor in your pulpit or your homes when you needed him. And I suppose no church in Brooklyn has ever been subjected to less strain than this one. Now you are called upon to face a new condition of things, perhaps a new danger—certainly a new duty. The duty overrides the danger. To meet that duty, you are strong in numbers . . . You are strong in a holy harmony. Let no man, no woman, break the ranks! You are strong in the protection of that great Shepherd who never resigns and who never grows old. "Lo! I am with you always! Lo! I am with you always! Lo! I am with you always!" (Matt 28:20) seems to greet me this morning from every wall of this sanctuary. I confidently expect to see Lafayette Avenue Church move steadily forward with unbroken column led by the Captain of our salvation. All eyes are upon you. The eye that never slumbers or sleeps is watching over you. If you are all true to conscience, true to your covenants, true to Christ, the future of this dear church may be as glorious as its past. And when another thirty years have rolled away, it may still be a strong tower of the truth on which the smile of God shall rest like the light of the morning. By as much as you love me, I entreat you not to sadden my life or break my heart by ever deserting these walls or letting the fire of devotion burn down on these sacred altars.

The hands of the clock warn me to close. This is one of the most trying hours of my whole life. It is an hour when tears are only endurable by being rainbowed with the memory of tender mercies and holy joys. When my feet descend those steps today, this will no longer be my pulpit. I surrender it back before God into your hands. One of my chiefest sorrows is that I leave some of my beloved hearers out of Christ. Oh, you have been faithfully warned here, and you have been lovingly invited here; and once more, as though God did beseech you by me, I implore you in Christ's name to be reconciled to God. This dear pulpit, whose teachings are based on the Rock of Ages, will stand long after the lips that now address you have turned to dust. It will be visible from the judgment seat; and its witness will be that I determined to know not anything among you save Jesus Christ and Him crucified (1 Cor 2:2). Today I write the last page in the record of thirty bright, happy, heaven-blessed years among you. What is written is written. I shall fold up the book and lay it away with all its many faults; and it will not lose its fragrance while between its leaves are the pressed flowers of your love. When my closing eyes shall look on that record for the last time, I hope to discover there only one name—the name that is above every name, the name of Him whose glory crowns this Easter morn with radiant splendor, the name of Jesus Christ, King of kings, Lord of lords. And the last words I utter in this sacred spot are unto Him that loves us and delivers us from sin with His precious blood; and unto God be all the praise and thanks and dominion and glory for ever and ever. Amen.

www.ingramcontent.com/pod-product-compliance
Lightning Source LLC
Chambersburg PA
CBHW052200090426
42741CB00010B/2347